Cromosys Publication

Delhi Killings

Niranjan Jha Showman

Founder - Niranjan Jha Showman

Corporation

Education and Technology Research Center

Patankar Park, Nallasopara (W), Mumbai. +91-9561450045

Education, Technology, Publication, Healthcare, Newsmedia, Realtor, Filmmaking

www.facebook.com/cromosys

+91-9561450045
Learn Advanced Skills
And Get Job Instantly
GERMAN
Python
FRENCH
C++
SPANISH
Java
ENGLISH
HTML5
RUSSIAN
CSS
JavaScript
Cromosys
Education and Technology Research Center
Nallasopara (W), Mumbai

Learn Web Programming
Demo-Class Free
HTML
CSS
React
JavaScript
Typescript
Bootstrap
Cromosys
20 Years of Experience
Nallasopara (W), Mumbai
+91-9561450045

+91-9561450045

Learn Software Engineering

Demo-Class Free

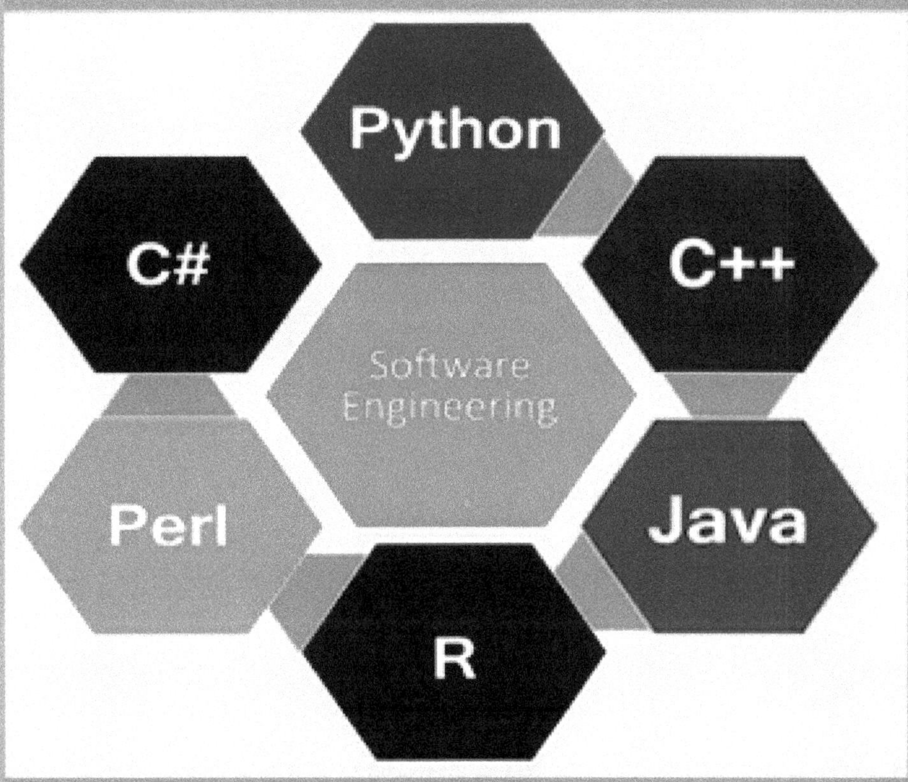

Python
C#
C++
Software
Engineering
Perl
Java
R

Cromosys
20 Years of Experience
Nallasopara (W), Mumbai
+91-9561450045

25 Years of Experience
Learn Visual Multimedia
Animation VFX
Movie Editing
Game Development
Cromosys
+91-9561450045
Education and Technology Research Center
Nallasopara (W), Mumbai
www.facebook.com/cromosys

Jobs Available
For Candidates Who Know

German

French

Spanish

Vacancy in Germany, France, Spain

For Hospitality, Engineering, IT Sector
With Free Visa, Airfare and Accommodation

Cromosys
Education and Technology Research Centre
Nallasopara (W), Mumbai
+91-9561450045
20 Years of Experience

+91-9561450045
Foreign Languages Institute
German, French, Spanish
Basic and Advanced - All Levels
3 x 6 = 18 Courses
FRANCHISE
Business Offer
Teaching Materials Provided
We have 1 Million Students Globally
Great Income Assured
Global Exposure
Cromosys
20 Years of Experience
Nallasopara (W), Mumbai
+91-9561450045

Cromosys Publication

Delhi Killings

Niranjan Jha Showman

"Hurting with truth is better than comforting with lies."
~ niranjan showman

Preface

The 2020 Delhi riots were multiple waves of bloodshed, property destruction, and rioting in North East Delhi, beginning on 23 February 2020 and caused chiefly by Hindu mobs attacking Muslims. Of the 53 people killed, two-thirds were Muslims who were shot, slashed with repeated blows, or set on fire. The dead also included a policeman, an intelligence officer and over a dozen Hindus, who were shot or assaulted. More than a week after the violence had ended, hundreds of wounded were languishing in inadequately staffed medical facilities and corpses were being found in open drains. By mid-March many Muslims had remained missing.

Muslims were marked as targets for violence. In order to have their religion ascertained, Muslim males—who unlike Hindus are commonly circumcised—were at times forced to remove their lower garments before being brutalized. Among the injuries recorded in one hospital were lacerated genitals. The properties destroyed were disproportionately Muslim-owned and included four mosques, which were set ablaze by rioters. By the end of February, many Muslims had left these neighborhoods. Even in areas of Delhi untouched by the violence, some Muslims had left for their ancestral villages, fearful for their personal safety in India's capital.

About the Author

Niranjan Jha Showman
Trainer, Author, Physician, Entrepreneur, Filmmaker, Activist

Niranjan Jha Showman is a Language Scientist and Technical Researcher. He is the Award Winning author of more than fifty educational and fictional books at Amazon. He is one of the great-grandsons of the first President of India Dr. Rajendra Prasad. He is a Public Figure, and the globally - renowned Languages Trainer of French, Spanish, and German from past twenty years. Niranjan Jha Showman is an Entrepreneur and also works as a Filmmaker in India. Being the founder and owner of Cromosys Corporation - a company located in Mumbai, India, his company is excelling in the fields of Education, Technology, Publication, Newsmedia, Realtors, Banking, and Cinemascope from past fifteen years.

Niranjan Jha Showman's good-seller educational books and novels are appreciated worldwide. He has more than one million eBook buyers online, and more than one million learners are connected to him globally. One of his novels is critically acclaimed. He is the trainer of French, Spanish, German, English Voice and Accent, and Advanced Computer Education. He is also a political activist in India.

Niranjan Jha Showman is the man who came from rags to riches, he who knows how to turn the table, and he, whom you call the man of Midas-touch. He has observed lives from the Pandora of monkeys to the sanctuary of monks, not only down-to-earth but down-to-grave. He is a B. Com. graduate, and B. Ed. from Delhi University, and diploma holder in French, Spanish and German from America. You can watch his songs, movies, educational videos and many more things by typing "Niranjan Jha Showman" in Google.

Niranjan Jha Showman
+91-9561450045
cromosys@yahoo.com
Mumbai, India
facebook.com/cromosys

Statutory

This book with its content is the registered property of the author Niranjan Showman.
The author and his Cromosys Publication holds all necessary rights of this book.
The author does not claim this book to be true or untrue.

All the writing works that include all the educational, non-educational books, novels, and articles of the writer Niranjan Jha Showman, are the registered content under MAHENG12112/13/1/2009-TC and the endorsement no. 3244 28/5/2009 with the Ministry of Information and Broadcasting, Govt. of India. Any plagiarism in this regard will attract strict legal action. Any further publication or production of any of his books requires his written permission.

Chapter 1

Wisps of smoke still rise from torched vehicles and shops of North East Delhi. Streets littered with brickbats remain mute spectators to the maelstrom that ravaged these parts of the capital of India. Over four dozen people lost their lives, hundreds of others were injured while countless houses, shops and offices were burnt down or damaged in a mayhem that singed northeast Delhi since late evening on February 23 2020. Paramilitary forces, Rapid Action Forces, and Central Reserve Police Force were deployed amid allegations of inaction and even complicity of Delhi Police personnel in the clashes that hit hard areas such as Maujpur, Jafrabad, Chand Bagh, Karawal Nagar and Gokulpuri of Delhi.

The 2020 Delhi riots were multiple incidents of religiously driven bloodshed, property destruction, and rioting in North East Delhi, beginning on the night of 23 February 2020 and causing the deaths of 53 people, mostly Muslims, who were shot, cut with irregular blows or set afire. Among the killed were also a policeman, an intelligence officer, and over a dozen Hindus, who were shot or assaulted. More than a week after the violence ended, hundreds of wounded were languishing in inadequately staffed medical facilities and corpses were being found in open drains. The massacre was continued up to three days even when Donald Trump, the president of America was present in Delhi.

Muslims were described as having been targeted by the rioters in some instances, the witnesses accused the policemen of joining the rioters. In other instances, Muslim males who unlike Hindu males are commonly circumcised were forced to show their genitals for ascertaining their religion before they were brutalized. The properties destroyed were disproportionately Muslim-owned and included four mosques, which were set ablaze by rioters. Many Muslims have left these neighborhoods. Even in areas of India's capital untouched by the violence, some Muslims have left for their ancestral villages, unsure of their safety.

Earlier, in Jaffrabad, in North East Delhi, a sit-in by women against India's Citizenship (Amendment) Act, 2019 had begun on a stretch of the Seelampur–Jaffrabad–Maujpur road. On 23 February 2020, a leader of the ruling Bharatiya Janata Party (BJP), Kapil Mishra, demanded that Delhi Police clear the roads occupied by protesters, and threatened to forcefully end the protests if the police failed. By the next day, rioters wearing helmets and carrying sticks, stones, swords or pistols, and the saffron flags of Hindu nationalism had begun to rush violently into the neighborhood, while the police remained completely passive. Mobs, both Hindu and Muslim, took to shooting with their guns; most deaths have been attributed to gunfire. In the neighborhood of Shiv Vihar, groups of violent Hindu men attacked Muslim houses and businesses for three days, often firebombing them with gas cylinders and gutting them without any resistance from the police.

The Indian government swiftly characterized the violence to be spontaneous. The Delhi Police, which is directly overseen by India's central government, moved into the area in strength on 26 February 2020. The National Security Advisor of India, Ajit Doval, then visited the area. Three days after the violence had begun, Prime Minister Narendra Modi made an appeal for peace on Twitter. As of 7 March 2020, the police had registered 690 first information reports (FIRs) and arrested or detained around 2200 individuals involved in the violence. The police have been accused by the affected citizens, eyewitnesses, human rights organizations and Muslim leaders around the world of falling well short in protecting Muslim people of the capital.

The neighborhood between Jaffrabad and Maujpur has a mixed population of Hindus and Muslims. The people of that area demonstrated unity by guarding one another, barricading the neighborhood entrance, and preventing outside mobs and rioters from entering and disturbing the communal harmony that has existed there.

The reason of this communal violence in the protests that began across India in December 2019 in response to the passage of the Citizenship Amendment Act (CAA), which allows fast-tracked naturalization for immigrants from Pakistan, Bangladesh and Afghanistan belonging to six religions namely Hinduism, Sikhism, Christianity, Zoroastrianism, Jainism and Buddhism. The Act has been seen as discriminatory to Muslims and threatening to their existence in India when combined with the anticipated National Register of Citizens (NRC).

Several anti-CAA protests were held in New Delhi from December 2019. Some protesters burned vehicles and pelted stones at Security forces. In Shaheen Bagh, protesters blocked roads, which led to a traffic jam in the surrounding area.

The Delhi Legislative Assembly election was held on 8 February 2020, in which the Bharatiya Janata Party (BJP) was defeated by the Aam Admi Party; widespread usage of incendiary slogans by BJP equating the protesters to anti-national elements and asking for them to be shot were noted. Delhi BJP chief, Manoj Tiwari has since attributed hate speeches by fellow party-candidate Kapil Mishra who coined the slogans as a cause of the BJP defeat.

On 22 February, around 500 to 1,000 protesters, including women, began a sit-in protest near the Jaffrabad metro station. The protest blocked a stretch of Seelampur–Jaffrabad–Maujpur road, as well as the entry and exit to the metro station. According to the protesters, the sit-in was in solidarity with the Bharat Bandh called by the Bhim Army, which was scheduled to begin on 23 February. Police and paramilitary personnel were deployed at the site.

Chapter 2

On 23 February between 3.30 and 4 pm, BJP leader Kapil Mishra and his supporters reached a protest site at Maujpur Chowk "to give an answer to Jaffrabad blockade". Mishra then spoke out in a rally against the CAA protesters and threatened to take matters into his own hands if the police failed to disperse the protesters from the Jaffrabad and Chand Bagh areas in three days. This has been widely reported to be the major inciting factor, however, Mishra rejects the allegations.

At approximately 4 pm, protesters were reported to have hurled stones at the pro-CAA gathering at Maujpur Chowk and near a temple. Between 9 to 11 pm, clashes broke out between the anti-CAA and pro-CAA demonstrators in Karawal Nagar, Maujpur Chowk, Babarpur and Chand Bagh. Vehicles were gutted and shops were destroyed. The police used baton charge and tear gas to disperse the crowd.

On the morning of 24 February, a pro-CAA mob arrived at an anti-CAA protest site at Jaffrabad and refused to leave until the anti-CAA protesters left the area. At around 12:30 pm, protesters wearing masks and waving swords clashed with the police force. By afternoon, violent clashes broke out in several areas of North East Delhi, including in the Gokulpuri and Kardampuri areas.

There was heavy stone pelting and vandalism of property. The police used tear gas and baton charge against the protesters in the Chand Bagh area, but the protesters retaliated by throwing stones at the police. A head constable, Ratan Lal, died of a bullet injury in this clash.

In Bhajanpura, in afternoon a group numbering around 2000 attacked a petrol pump, chanting slogans of Freedom, and carrying petrol bombs, sticks and weapons. They attacked the owner and employees of the petrol pump with sticks, burning vehicles and petrol tanks after looting available cash.

Violence was also reported from the areas of Seelampur, Jaffrabad, Maujpur, Kardampuri, Babarpur, Gokulpuri and Shivpuri. Section 144, which is a ban on assembly, was imposed in all the affected areas but to little effect. In Jaffrabad, a man, allegedly linked with the anti-CAA side, opened fire at the police, before being arrested days later in Uttar Pradesh.

In Shiv Vihar, in the afternoon, several shops and homes owned by Hindus were torched by a Muslim mob. Later, mutilated bodies of workers were recovered from the site. A massive parking lot with 170 cars was burned by a mob. In the evening around 8:30 pm, a tyre market owned by Muslims was set on fire with the screaming of "Hail Lord Rama" being heard. Later that night, at around 10:30 pm, a mob beat Monu Kumar and his father Vinod Kumar with sticks, stones and swords while screaming "Allahu akbar". Vinod Kumar died on the spot. On that day, five people died including a police constable and four civilians.

Three thousand five hundred emergency calls were made to the police control room that day. The Delhi Fire Service stated that it had attended 45 calls from areas in northeast Delhi and three firemen were injured, on 24 February. While attending calls, a fire engine was attacked with stones, while another fire engine was set on fire by rioters.

On 25 February, stone pelting was reported from Maujpur, Brahampuri and other neighboring areas. Around 5 am in Brahmpuri, Atul Kumar was shot during a morning walk. Rapid Action Force were deployed in the worst affected areas. It was a full-blown riot with intense religious sloganeering and violence from both sides.

In Ashok Nagar, a mosque was vandalized and a Hanuman flag was placed on one of the minarets of the mosque. It was also reported that prayer mats of the mosque were burnt and torn pages from the Quran were strewn outside the mosque. A mob sloganeering "Hail Lord Rama" marched around the mosque before setting it on fire and looting adjacent shops and houses. According to local residents, the attackers did not belong to the area. After the first wave of violence by rioters, the police evacuated Muslim residents and took them to the police station. While the residents were away, a second mosque in Ashok Nagar and a third in Brijpuri were also torched along with a three-story house and eight shops in the vicinity; the rioters could not be identified.

At 3 pm in Durgapuri, Hindu and Muslim mobs clashed, pelting stones and shooting at each other. The rioters shouted religious slogans whilst shops and vehicles belonging to Muslims were exclusively torched. Police were not present initially in the area and arrived almost an hour later. At Gamri extension, a Hindu mob attacked a lane, and an 85-year-old woman was burnt to death when her house was set on fire. In Karawal Nagar, acid was thrown by protesters on the paramilitary personnel, who were deployed in the area to maintain law and order. People wielding sticks and iron rods were reported to be roaming streets in the areas.

By 9:30 pm, it was reported that 13 people died due to violence. Among the injured, more than 70 people suffered gunshot injuries. At 10 pm, shoot at sight orders were given to police in the riot-affected area. The dead body of Ankit Sharma, a trainee driver in the Intelligence Bureau at Chanakyapuri, was found in a drain in Jaffrabad, a day after he went missing. The circumstances leading to his death are under investigation with a lot of confusion regarding them. According to a post-mortem report, he was repeatedly stabbed, leading to his death. Tahir Hussain, who was an Aam Aadmi Party (AAP) councilor, was arrested for allegedly murdering Sharma.

Seven thousand five hundred emergency calls were made to the police control room throughout the day, the highest in the week. The National Security Advisor of India, Ajit Doval, visited violence-affected areas of North East Delhi in the evening. However, reports of violence, arson and mob lynching emerged from Karawal Nagar, Maujpur and Bhajanpura later that night.

The complaints of delayed post-mortem reports were aired from several hospitals while witnesses and affected individuals who claimed to be civilians gave statements. Some of them blamed Kapil Mishra for the riots while one individual stated that a mob attacked them with stones and swords while chanting the religious slogans.

Chapter 3

On 27 February, in Shiv Vihar, between 7 and 9 am, clashes were reported. Three injured persons were reported, one of whom had bullet wounds. A warehouse, two shops, and a motorcycle were torched. On 28 February, a 60-year-old rag picker, who had stepped out of home assuming the situation had normalized, was attacked and died on way to the hospital due to head injuries.

On 29 February, with no fresh cases of violence reported to the police on the day, the situation was said to be returning to normal with some shops reopening. Thirteen cases were registered against people posting provocative content on social media.

On 1 March, in the Welcome area, one shop was set on fire. Meanwhile, rumors of further violence were circulated on social media, following which the Delhi Police announced that the situation was peaceful. Seven metro stations that includes Nawada, Nangloi, Tughlakabad, Tilak Nagar, Badarpur, Surajmal Stadium and Uttam Nagar West were closed for an hour due to the panic caused by the rumors.

During this violence, several incidents of mobs attacking journalists were reported during the riots. A journalist of JK News was shot by Anti-CAA protestors on 25 February while reporting in the Maujpur area. Two journalists of NDTV along with a cameraman were attacked by the mob while they were recording the torching of a mosque in the area. One of the journalists sustained severe injuries. A journalist involved in the same incident had to intervene and convince the mob that the journalists were Hindus to save them from further assault.

On 25 February, a photojournalist who worked for The Times of India was heckled by the Hindu Sena members while taking pictures of a building that had been set on fire. The group tried to put a mark on his forehead. The group also claimed that it will make his job easier as he could then be identified as a Hindu by the rioters.

They questioned his intentions of taking pictures of the building on fire and further threatened to remove his pants to reveal that he is not circumcised, as an evidence of being a Hindu. The reporter was later approached by another rioter who demanded him to prove his religion.

Several journalists shared their experience with rioters on Twitter. A journalist of Times Now tweeted that she was attacked by pro-CAA and right-wing protesters. She said that she had to plead with the mob, who were carrying stones and sticks, to escape from the site. Journalists of Reuters, India Today, CNN-News too stated that they were assaulted.

The Hindustan Times reported that a motorcycle, which belonged to one of its photographers who was documenting the violence in Karawal Nagar, was set on fire by a masked mob. After torching the motorcycle, the mob threatened, assaulted him and seized the memory card of his camera. They asked for his official identity card and took a photograph of it before letting him leave.

The Editors Guild of India issued a statement on 25 February expressing concern about the attacks on journalists as an assault on freedom of the press in India. They urged the Home Ministry and the Delhi Police to investigate the incidents and bring the perpetrators to justice.

The-Print journalists, who covered the incidents, reported that the people of the localities were confident that their neighbors did not engage in violence against them. Rather they blamed the "outsiders". The neighborhood between Jaffrabad and Maujpur, which has a mixed population of Hindus and Muslims, demonstrated unity by guarding one another and barricading the gate to prevent outside mobs from entering and destroying the communal harmony that exists there. In the area of Mustafabad, Hindus and Muslims joined together to keep guard to prevent miscreants to enter the area.

Some Hindu families worked to protect their Muslim friends and neighbors amidst the riots by inviting them into their homes for a few days until the riots calmed down. Premkanth Baghel, a local Hindu, rescued his Muslim friends from their burning house. He himself got burnt up to seventy percent while rescuing them. In the area of Chand Bagh, some Muslims visited their Hindu neighbors and assured their safety. At the Mandir Masjid Marg of Noor-e-Ilahi, Muslims gathered around Hanuman Mandir, the Hindu temple, to protect it from being damaged while Hindus did the same for Azizya Masjid, a mosque in the same area.

Mohinder Singh and his son Inderjit Singh rescued around seventy Muslims from a mosque and a madrasa that were surrounded by a mob, by transporting them to safety on their motorcycle, giving safe passage to two children at a time. Akali Dal leader and former MLA, Majinder Singh Sirsa, opened up his shrine to those seeking shelter amidst the rioting.

The Delhi Police's ability to maintain the law and order and bring the peace back in riot-affected areas has been questioned by multiple sources. The police took no action even though present when the violence resulted in murders. They remained lax in deploying policemen on 23 February, when multiple intelligence reports requested more forces to prevent the tense situation created by Mishra's speech from escalating further. Victims of the riot reported that the police did not respond promptly when called, claiming that the officers were busy. Other reports also suggested that the police encouraged rioters and physically attacked residents of riot-affected areas, going on to shoot people randomly. The police, however, denied these assertions.

Some news channels did not show the truth and some did not get access to the affected place. A video was widely shared on social media on 26 February. It showed a group of men being assaulted by the local police as they lay on the ground. They are forcibly singing the national anthem of India on the demands of the policemen.

The victims spoke to the media next day. They claimed that they were detained in the lockup for two days. They were also beaten further. One of them, Faizan, was admitted in the neurosurgery wing of LNJP Hospital. But he died on 29 February from critical gunshot wounds of police. Another was reported to have suffered serious injuries.

Chapter 4

The lack of the police's prompt response may be attributed to the large police force deployed to line the roads for the visit of the United States President Donald Trump. The police had reportedly informed the Ministry of Home Affairs of the shortfall of policeman available for immediately controlling the violence, but this was denied by the Ministry.

When the Delhi High Court bench, on 27 February, ordered the Delhi Police to file FIRs against the people whose speeches triggered the riots, the police and the government remarked that they had consciously not done so, citing that arresting them would not restore immediate peace. They further informed the court that they would need more time to investigate the matter.

When a team of lawyers visited Jagatpuri police station to visit the anti-CAA protestors detained by the police, they were reportedly abused by police personnel. The lawyers then wrote to the Delhi commissioner of police, demanding action against the officer who assaulted them in the Jagatpuri police station that day.

The Jan Swasthya Abhiyaan (JSA), a public health advocacy group, compiled a report on the information gathered by their volunteers working in the hospitals during the riots. The report, titled The Role of Health Systems in Responding to Communal Violence in Delhi that was released on 2 March. The report alleged that doctors had harassed the victims by referring to them as terrorists, and had asked victims if they knew the full forms of "NRC" and "CAA".

The report documented instances of negligence, denying victims treatment in some cases, while disregarding the safety of patients in others. Multiple cases were reportedly rejected for not having the required medico legal case documentation. It was also alleged that the doctors did not provide detailed reports of the injuries and autopsies to the victims and their families.

The report indicated that citizens had grown fearful of government services such as ambulances and government hospitals, with victims taking private vehicles to go to private hospitals, due to the treatment and abuse that they had received from the police. This problem compounded the existing issues of the mobs not allowing ambulances near the riot-affected areas. In some areas, primary health centers and hospitals remained closed throughout the riots, either due to the violence or due to lack of medical facilities available at the grassroots level even before the riots began. Families of the victims also reported delayed post-mortem reports from several hospitals.

The Delhi Government run by AAP Party could not do much. On 25 February, the newly elected Chief Minister of Delhi, Arvind Kejriwal stated that the Police, despite its efforts, had been unable to control the violence and requested the Army's assistance in stopping the violence as the number of deaths climbed to 23 at the end of that day.

At a rally in Delhi, a Union Cabinet minister shouted:
"What's to be done with the traitors to the nation?"

And the crowd screamed back:
"Shoot the bastards!"

AAP leader Sanjay Singh released a video in which BJP MLA from Laxmi Nagar, Abhay Verma, was seen leading crowds that raised slogans:
"Whoever talks about the welfare of Hindus, only they will rule the country."

Sanjay Singh accused Home Minister Amit Shah of holding an all-party meeting, pretending to restore peace and their MLA is engaged in inciting riots. Verma meanwhile defended himself claiming the slogans were raised by civilians.

Indian National Congress president Sonia Gandhi held a press conference at which she said that Shah should resign for failing to stop the violence. She asked for the deployment of an adequate number of security forces. Gandhi's press conference was followed by a press conference by Prakash Javadekar; he said that there is "selective silence" from AAP and Congress and he added that they are politicizing violence.

After three days of violence with 40 deaths, the Prime Minister of India, Narendra Modi, shared a message on Twitter asking people to maintain peace. Commentators said that he reacted only after the departure of President Trump, whom he had been hosting on a state visit while the riots began.

On 26 February, the US Commission on International Religious Freedom (USCIRF) conveyed "grave concern" over the riots and requested the Indian government to provide protection to people, no matter which faith they belonged to. The US Senator and 2020 US presidential candidate Bernie Sanders and other American politicians expressed their concerns over the events.

In response, on 27 February 2020, the Ministry of External Affairs spokesperson, Raveesh Kumar, stated that these remarks were "factually inaccurate", "misleading" and "aimed at politicizing the issue". The BJP general secretary BL Santhosh threatened Sanders with election interference due to his condemnation. The US issued a travel advisory for its citizens to exercise caution.

On 27 February, United Nations High Commissioner for Human Rights, Michelle Bachelet, stated, "Indians in huge numbers, and from all communities, have expressed—in a mostly peaceful manner—their opposition to the Act, and support for the country's long tradition of secularism,". She expressed concern on the citizenship law and reports of "police inaction" during the communal attacks in Delhi. Twelve eminent citizens of Bangladesh also expressed grave concern over the communal clashes on that day. They expressed fear that India's failure to handle the situation could create a volatile environment in its neighboring countries, which could destroy peace, democracy and development in the region.

On 27 February, Turkish president Erdogan also criticized the Delhi violence. He said, "India right now has become a country where massacres are widespread. What massacres? Massacres of Muslims. By whom? By Hindu people." Erdogan also alleged the Indian religious fundamentalist to bring the Muslim community in fear. Some Indian political authorities said that he personally does not like Donald Trump, and his visit to India, so he said so.

 On 2 March, the Chief Minister of West Bengal, Mamata Banerjee, alleged that the Delhi riot was a planned genocide. On 5th March, Supreme Leader of Iran, Ayatollah Ali Khamenei, asked the Indian Government to confront extremist Hindus and their parties and stop the massacre of Muslims of India, to prevent India from being isolated from the world of Islam.

On 24 February 2020, the Indian Ministry of Home Affairs stated that the violence appeared orchestrated to coincide with President Donald Trump's February 24–25, 2020 visit to India. The Ministry also refused to bring in the Army to control the riots and stated that the number of central forces and policemen on the ground was adequate. The Ministry said that more than 6,000 police and paramilitary personnel were deployed in the area.

Chapter 5

On the morning of 25 February 2020, the Chief Minister Arvind Kejriwal chaired an urgent meeting of all party MLAs from the violence-hit areas and senior officials. Several MLAs raised concerns on the lack of deployment of enough policemen. The concerns were raised by Kejriwal in the subsequent meeting chaired by Home Minister Shah and attended by Delhi Lieutenant-Governor Anil Baijal and senior police officials. The meeting concluded with the decision to take all possible steps to contain violence. Kejriwal stated that Shah had assured the availability of an adequate number of policemen.

By the Home Ministry, the National Security Advisor Ajit Doval was given the responsibility of restoring peace in the region. On 26 February, Doval travelled to the violence-hit regions and spoke to locals, assuring them of normalcy. He also said, "Let the past bygone." But he did not give any assurance of taking action on the miscreants

On 27 February, Kejriwal announced free treatment for the injured in government as well as private hospitals under the Government scheme. The government had made arrangements with the help of NGOs to supply food in areas where a curfew had been imposed. He also announced a compensation amount. He also announced that the Delhi government had set up nine shelters for the people affected by the riots. For people whose houses were completely burnt, immediate assistance was announced.

Food, water, clothes and other relief materials were distributed with the help of resident welfare associations and NGOs of Delhi. The BJP leaders Tajinder Bagga and Kapil Mishra collected 1 million rupees for the Hindu victims via crowd-funding. On 27 February 2020, Delhi Police reported that two Special Investigation Teams (SIT) had been formed to investigate the violence in the city. DCP Joy Tirkey and DCP Rajesh Deo were appointed head of these SITs respectively, along with four Assistant Commissioners in each team. Additional Commissioner of crime branch, B.K. Singh is supervising the work of the SITs. On 28 February 2020, the police also informed forensic science teams who visited the crime scenes to collect evidence.

After a week, by 7 March 2020, police had registered 690 FIRs and around 2200 individuals involved in the violence were taken into custody. Some activists were charged with offences under Indian Penal code and the Arms Act. When the activists' friends and relatives spoke to the media, they alleged that they were tortured in custody.

The Bhim Army chief Chandrashekhar Azad Ravan came to Delhi next day. Chandrashekhar along with former Chief Information Commissioner Wajahat Habibullah and social activist Syed Bahadur Abbas Naqvi, filed an appeal in the Supreme Court seeking direction to the police to file reports over cases of violence that occurred since the night of 23 February. His petition also accused Mishra of "inciting and orchestrating the riots". The plea was filed through Advocate Mehmood Pracha, in an intervention in a matter relating to removal of protesters from the public road in Shaheen Bagh and is scheduled for hearing on 26 February.

On 26 February, while hearing the issue, the Supreme Court criticized Delhi Police for not doing enough to stop the inflammatory speech and the violence. The bench, consisting of Justices Sanjay Kishan Kaul and K. M. Joseph, slammed the police for lack of "professionalism" and questioned why the police had to wait for orders to act during such law and order situation. The court added that the violence could have been prevented if the police had taken the necessary action on the people who incited violence. The Supreme Court did not entertain any plea on the Delhi incidents as the case is being heard in the Delhi High Court.

A plea was filed in the Delhi High Court, seeking police reports and arrests of the people involved in the violence. It was to be received for an urgent hearing on 25 February. However, the court stated that the plea would be heard on 26 February. The plea filed by activists Harsh Mander and Farah Naqvi also asked for a Special Investigation Team (SIT) to investigate the incident, in addition to compensation for those killed and injured. It also requested for the deployment of the Indian Army to maintain law and order in the affected areas of Delhi.

At midnight on 26 February, the court bench consisting of Justices S. Muralidhar and Talwant Singh, heard the plea to provide the safe passage to the riot victims to reach their nearest government or private hospitals. Following this, the court ordered the police to safeguard and help all victims to reach their nearest hospitals. The bench also directed the police to submit a report of compliance that would include information about the injured victims and the treatments offered to them. The same was to be placed before the court for the following hearing date.

In the morning during the hearing, the court asked the DCP of crime branch, Rajesh Deo, and the Solicitor General of India, Tushar Mehta, if they had watched the inflammatory speech given by Kapil Mishra. In response, DCP Deo surprised the court by saying he did not watch the video of Mishra but watched videos of Anurag Thakur and Parvesh Verma. The Court then played the video clip of Kapil Mishra's speech, going on to direct the police to decide within 24 hours on filing cases related to the hate speeches made by the four BJP leaders, Kapil Mishra, Anurag Thakur, Parvesh Verma and Abhay Verma.

Justice S. Muralidhar expressed distress over the situation by criticizing the inability of police. The bench also expressed "anguish" over the failure of Delhi Police to control the riots and its failure to file FIRs against the BJP leaders for their hate speeches. It was noted that Delhi could not be allowed to repeat incidents like the 1984 anti-Sikh riots.

Late on the night of 26 February, Justice S. Muralidhar who presided over the plea hearing, was transferred to Punjab and Haryana High Court. He was transferred on the same day he condemned the Delhi Police for its failure in controlling the riots or filing cases against BJP leader for hate speech. However, official sources said this was a routine transfer which had been recommended by the Supreme Court a fortnight before.

BBC News reported that his "biting comments could have hastened his transfer". The news of his removal from the case was criticized by many Indians who expressed concern. The Congress party called his transfer a move to protect the accused BJP leaders involved in the massacre. The Delhi High Court Bar Association also criticized Justice S. Muralidhar transfer and asked the Supreme Court collegium to revoke it for the safeguard of justice.

On 27 February, the court resumed the hearing with a new bench consisting of Chief Justice D.N. Patel and Justice C. Hari Shankar. During the previous hearing, the Delhi police were given 24 hours to decide on the filing of FIRs over hate speeches by four BJP leaders. The government's lawyer claimed that the situation was not "conducive" and that the government needed more time before it could take appropriate action.

The new bench accepted the same arguments that the previous bench of Justice S. Muralidhar had rejected. The new bench agreed to give the government more time to decide on filing of the cases for hate speech. The petitioners' lawyer requested an earlier hearing, citing the increasing number of deaths, but the court set 13 April as the date of the next hearing.

On 28 February, the court issued notices to Delhi and central governments seeking their responses on registering FIRs on Congress party leaders Sonia Gandhi, Rahul Gandhi, and Priyanka Gandhi on the charges of delivering hate speeches. Hearing another plea, the bench also issued notice to Delhi police and central government for their response on registering FIR on AAP MLA Amanatullah Khan, actress Swara Bhaskar, activist Harsh Mander and on AIMIM leaders like Akbaruddin Owaisi, Asaduddin Owaisi, and Waris Pathan. The court later posted the matter to be heard again on 13 April.

Chapter 6

1927 Nagpur riots

The Nagpur riots of 1927 were part of series of riots taking place across various cities in British India during the 1920s. Nagpur was then the capital of Central Provinces and Berar (CP&B) state of British India which covered most of the central India. The riots occurred on 4 September 1927. On that day, there was a procession for Mahalakshmi, which is said to have been blocked by Muslims when it came to the Mahal neighborhood.

In the afternoon, there was rioting near the Hindu houses of the neighborhood, which continued for three days. The mutual trust between Hindu and Muslim communities had reached a low in the 1920s, and riots were seen frequently across many cities of India. In 1923, India witnessed eleven riots, in 1924 there were eighteen riots, in 1925 there were sixteen riots, and in 1926 there were thirty five riots. In the twelve months from May 1926 to April 1926, 40 more riots occurred across various cities.

They mostly occurred in Bengal, Punjab and United Provinces (UP). Lahore riots of August 1927 were the most deadly recorded riots in this series. The earlier riot of 1923 was caused when the members of Hindu Mahasabha took out a procession and passed in front of a mosque, playing loud music. The Muslim community objected, starting a skirmish between the two parties. These riots had a profound impact on K. B. Hedgewar, prompting him to form, in 1925, the Rashtriya Swayamsevak Sangh (RSS), a Hindu nationalist organization and one of the largest Hindu organizations in the world.

Christophe Jaffrelot in his book The Hindu Nationalist Movement and Indian Politics records a testimony saying that Hedgewar led the Ganesha procession in 1927, beating the drums in defiance of the usual practice not to pass in front of the mosque with music. All these events acted as a catalyst building up the tensions between two communities.

On the morning of 4 September, the day of Lakshmi Puja, Hindus took out a procession like every year, and passed in front of a mosque in the Mahal area of Nagpur. However, the Muslims stopped the procession this time around and did not allow it to pass through the area. In the afternoon, when the Hindus were resting after the morning procession, Muslim youths took out a procession shouting Allahu Akbar, armed with weapons like javelins, daggers and knives.

Muslim youths threw stones at the house of Hedgewar, who was then away from Nagpur. RSS cadres, sensing the mood of the procession, came out in the narrow lanes of the Mahal area and reciprocated with lathis, further intensifying the riots. Liaquat Ali Khan, in his book Pakistan – The Heart of Asia, also describes a major arson incident during the riot that seemed pre-meditated with explosives gathered well before the riots began.

The Washington Post reported 22 had been killed and more than 100 injured in riots that continued for two days. Later, the government ordered troops into the city to restore peace. During the riots, the RSS had grouped its cadres in 16 shakhas, spread out across the city to protect the Hindu communities.

RSS had showcased its role in defending Hindus during the riots. The popularity of the organization grew as the news of the incident spread across the country, and it saw a spurt in its membership. By 1929, the organization formed an elaborate hierarchical structure. Between 1931 and 1939, the number of its branches grew from 60 to 500. The membership count had reached 60,000 by this time.

Chapter 7

1969 Gujarat riots
The 1969 Gujarat riots refers to the communal violence between Hindus and Muslims during September–October 1969, in Gujarat, India. The violence was Gujarat's first major riot that involved massacre, arson and looting on a large scale. It was the most deadly Hindu-Muslim violence since the 1947 partition of India, and remained so until the 1989 Bhagalpur violence.

According to the official figures, 660 people were killed, 1074 people were injured and over 48,000 lost their property. Unofficial reports claim as high as 2000 deaths. The Muslim community suffered the majority of the losses. Out of the 512 deaths reported in the police complaints, 430 were Muslims.

Property worth 42 million rupees was destroyed during the riots, with Muslims losing 32 million worth of property. A distinctive feature of the violence was the attack on Muslim chawls by their Dalit Hindu neighbors who had maintained peaceful relations with them until this point.

The riots happened during the chief ministership of the Indian National Congress leader Hitendra Desai. The Justice Reddy Commission set up by his government blamed the Hindu nationalist organizations for instigating the violence. Various writers trace the causes of the riots to a mix of socioeconomic and political factors.

The violence started on 18 September 1969 after Muslims attacked some Hindu sadhus and a temple, after the cows herded by the sadhus caused injury to them. The Hindus later attacked a Muslim dargah, and Muslim protesters also attacked the temple again, leading to a mass breakout of violence. The riots started in Ahmedabad, and then spread to other areas, notably Vadodara, Mehsana, Nadiad, Anand and Gondal. By 26 September, the violence had been brought under control, however some more violent incidents happened during 18–28 October 1969.

The Hindu-Muslim tension increased considerably in Gujarat during the 1960s. Between 1961 and 1971, there were 685 incidents of communal violence in the urban areas of Gujarat (plus, another 114 in the rural areas). Out of the 685 incidents, 578 incidents happened in 1969 alone. Although Ahmedabad had been divided along the caste and religious lines, it was not a communally sensitive area until the 1960s.

In the 1960s, the city's textile mills attracted a large number of migrants from other parts of the state. During 1961-71, the city's population grew by nearly 38%, resulting in rapid growth of slums in the eastern part of the city. However, mid-1960s onwards, a number of under-qualified mill workers in Ahmedabad became unemployed, as the jobs went to the small units of Surat. During the 1960s, seven large mills in Ahmedabad shut down, and around 17,000 workers lost their jobs. The Hindus were over-represented among these workers, compared to the Muslims. The Dalit Hindu workers faced a greater sense of insecurity, as the local Muslim workers were said to be more skilled in the weaving.

Several violent clashes involving the textile workers took place in the slums of the city, mainly between the Hindu Dalits and the Muslims. The changing socioeconomic factors also impacted the political situation in the city. The Indian National Congress had been fragmenting, leading to tensions between its factions: the Congress eventually split into Congress (O) and Congress (I) in 1969. At the same time, the Hindu nationalist organization Rashtriya Swayamsevak Sangh (RSS) had established local strongholds in the eastern parts of the city.

Several incidents led to increase in tensions between the two communities in Ahmedabad. During a three-day rally held in Maninagar during 27–28 December 1968, the RSS supremo M. S. Golwalkar pleaded for a Hindu Rashtra ("Hindu nation"). On the Muslim side, provocative speeches were made at the conference of Jamiat Ulema-e-Hind in June 1969.

On the evening of 3 March 1969, a Hindu police officer moved a handcart that was obstructing traffic near the Kalupur Tower. A copy of Koran placed on the handcart fell on the ground, resulting in a demand for an apology by a small Muslim crowd standing nearby. The crowd soon grew bigger, and twelve policemen were injured in the subsequent violent protests. On 31 August, the Muslims of the city held a massive demonstration to protest the burning of the Al-Aqsa Mosque in Jerusalem.

On 4 September, a Muslim sub-inspector, while dispersing a Ramlila festive crowd, hit a table. As a result, the Hindu text Ramayana and an Aarti thali (plate) fell down. The Hindus alleged that the police officer also kicked the sacred book. This incident led to protests by Hindus, and the formation of the Hindu Dharma Raksha Samiti by the RSS leaders. The Hindu Dharma Raksha Samiti ("Hindu Religion Protection Committee") organized protests in which anti-Muslim slogans were raised. The Bharatiya Jana Sangh leader Balraj Madhok visited the city and made fiery speeches on 14 and 15 September. Another incident included an alleged assault on some Muslim maulvis, who were trying to construct a mosque in the Odhav village near Ahmedabad.

On 18 September 1969, a Muslim crowd had gathered in the Jamalpur area of Ahmedabad to celebrate the local Urs festival at the tomb of a Sufi saint (Bukhari Saheb's Chilla). When the sadhus (Hindu holy men) of the nearby Jagannath temple tried to bring their cows back to the temple compound through the crowded streets, some Muslim women were injured. The cows also allegedly damaged some carts on which the Muslims were selling goods. This led to violence in which some Muslim youths attacked and injured the sadhus, and damaged the temple windows. Sevadasji, the mahant (priest) of the Hindu temple, went on a protest fast, which he gave up after a 15-member Muslim delegation led by A.M. Peerzada met him and apologized.

However, subsequently, a dargah (tomb shrine) near the temple was damaged by some Hindus. A large number of Muslims protestors gathered in the area. On the afternoon of 19 September, a crowd of 2500-3000 Muslims attacked the temple again. Following this, the rumors spread and the violence escalated, resulting in several incidents of arson, murders and attacks on the places of worship around the area. The Muslims in the eastern areas of the city and its suburbs started fleeing their homes for safer areas. Several trains carrying them were stopped and attacked. A curfew was imposed on the evening of 19 September, and on the next day, the army was called in to control the violence.

During 19–24 September, 514 people were killed. This period also saw damage to 6,123 houses and shops, mainly by Hindus. In the afternoon of 20 September 1969, a young Muslim man, angry at the destruction of his property by Hindus, announced that he would take revenge. An angry Hindu mob beat him up and asked him to shout Jai Jagannath ("Hail Jagannath"). The Muslim man said that he would rather die. The crowd then sprinkled petrol on him and burnt him to death. The municipal corporation by-election scheduled for 22 September was postponed. The first curfew relaxation on the next day resulted in 30 deaths within the first 3 hours.

After a year of time, according to the Justice Reddy Commission set up by the Congress Government to investigate the riots, the Hindu nationalist organizations like RSS, Hindu Mahasabha and Jan Sangh were involved in the riots. The Justice Jaganmohan Reddy Commission of Enquiry was set up by the Government of Gujarat's Home Department. It published a seventeen page report in the year of 1971, questioning the police's role in the riots.

It found around six instances of Muslim religious places adjoining police lines or police stations being attacked or damaged. The police defended themselves claiming these police stations did not have adequate strength since the forces were busy quelling the riots at other places. However, the commission refused to entertain this argument, since there was no report of damage to a Hindu place of worship near any police station. Overall, 37 mosques, 50 dargahs, 6 kabristans (Muslim graveyards) and 3 temples were destroyed.

The journalist Ajit Bhattacharjea accused the police of not taking any "firm action for the first three days", and stated that "this was not a matter of slackness but policy". An unnamed senior Congress leader told him that their government was reluctant to use force because it was afraid of losing power to Jan Sangh in the next elections in case it did so.

The members of the Bharatiya Jana Sangh called the violence a revenge for the massacre of Hindus by the Muslim League in 1946.[citation needed] On 26 September, a Hindu organization called Sangram Samiti claimed that the Congress-led government had been appeasing the Muslims, and had been encouraging the "abolition of Hindu religion under the name of secularism". The Hindu organizations claimed that after the alleged desecration of the Koran in March, the Hindu police officer had to apologize twice, while "it took days for taking any steps when the Hindus were similarly insulted" after the alleged desecration of the Ramayana in September.

According to the author and social activist Achyut Yagnik, the 1969 riots were a turning point in the Hindu-Muslim relations in Gujarat, and led to a drop in the tolerance levels, which was visible in the later riots of 1992-93 and 2002. After the 1969 riots, the state saw increasing Muslim ghettoization.

According to the Hindustan Times report in 2011, the violence was "deliberately engineered" to discredit the chief minister Hitendra Desai, who had been supporting the Congress (O) leader Morarji Desai instead of the Congress (I) leader Indira Gandhi.

Chapter 8

1984 anti-Sikh riots
The 1984 anti-Sikh riots, also known as the 1984 Sikh Massacre, was a series of organized pogroms against Sikhs in India in response to the assassination of Indira Gandhi by her Sikh bodyguards. The ruling Indian National Congress had been in active complicity with the mob, as to the organization of the riots. Government estimates project that about 2,800 Sikhs were killed in Delhi and 3,350 nationwide, whilst independent sources estimate the number of deaths at about 8,000–17,000.

The violence continued in the early 1980s in Punjab because of the armed Sikh separatist Khalistan movement which sought independence from India. In July 1982, the Sikh political party Akali Dal's President Harchand Singh Longowal had invited Jarnail Singh Bhindranwale to take up residence in Golden Temple Complex to evade arrest.

Jarnail Singh Bhindranwale later on made the sacred temple complex an armory and headquarters for his separatist movement of Punjab. In the violent events leading up to the Operation Blue Star since the inception of Akali Dharm Yudh Morcha, the militants had killed 165 Hindus and Nirankaris, even 39 Sikhs opposed to Bhindranwale were killed. The total number of deaths was 410 in violent incidents and riots while 1,180 people were injured. Operation Blue Star was an Indian military operation carried out between 1 and 8 June 1984, ordered by Prime Minister Indira Gandhi to remove militant religious leader Jarnail Singh Bhindranwale and his armed militants from the buildings of the Harmandir Sahib complex in Amritsar, Punjab.

Bhindranwale died and militants were removed from the temple complex. The military action in the temple complex was criticized by Sikhs worldwide who had interpreted it as an assault on Sikh religion. Four months after the operation, on 31 October 1984, Indira Gandhi was assassinated in vengeance by her two Sikh bodyguards, Satwant Singh and Beant Singh, who shot Indira Gandhi 33 times.

Public outcry over Gandhi's death led to the killings of Sikhs in the ensuing riots. In the aftermath of the riots, the government reported that 20,000 had fled the city; the People's Union for Civil Liberties reported "at least" 1,000 displaced persons. The most-affected regions were the Sikh neighborhoods of Delhi.

Human rights organizations and newspapers across India believed that the massacre was organized. The collusion of political officials in the violence and judicial failure to penalize the perpetrators alienated Sikhs and increased support for the Khalistan movement. The Akal Takht, Sikhism's governing body, considers the killings genocide.

In 2011, Human Rights Watch reported that the Government of India had "yet to prosecute those responsible for the mass killings". According to the 2011 WikiLeaks cable leaks, the United States was convinced of Indian National Congress' complicity in the riots and called it "opportunism" and "hatred" by the Congress government, of Sikhs. Although the U.S. has not identified the riots as genocide, it acknowledged that "grave human rights violations" occurred.

In 2011, a new group of mass graves was discovered in Haryana and Human Rights Watch reported that "widespread anti-Sikh attacks in Haryana were part of broader revenge attacks" in India.The Central Bureau of Investigation, the main Indian investigative agency, believes that the violence was organized with support from the Delhi police and some central-government officials.

In 1972 Punjab state elections, Congress won and Akali Dal was defeated. In 1973, Akali Dal put forward the Anandpur Sahib Resolution to demand more autonomy to Punjab. It demanded that power be generally given from the Central to state governments. The Congress government considered the resolution a secessionist document and rejected it. Bhindranwale then joined the Akali Dal to launch the Dharam Yudh Morcha in 1982 to implement the Anandpur Sahib resolution.

Bhindranwale had risen to prominence in the Sikh political circle with his policy of getting the Anandpur Resolution passed, failing which he wanted to declare a separate country of Khalistan as a homeland for Sikhs. Others demanded an autonomous state in India, based on the Anandpur Sahib Resolution. Many Sikhs condemned the militants' actions.

Bhindranwale symbolized the revivalist, extremist and terrorist movement in the 1980s in Punjab. He is credited with launching the Sikh militancy in Punjab. Under Bhindranwale, the number of people initiated into the Khalsa increased. He also increased the level of rhetoric on the perceived "assault" on Sikh values from the Hindu community. Bhindranwale and his followers started carrying firearms at all times. In 1983, to escape arrest, he along with his militant cadre occupied and fortified the Sikh shrine Akal Takht.

By 1983, the situation in Punjab was volatile. In October, Sikh militants stopped a bus and shot six Hindu passengers. On the same day, another group killed two officials on a train. The Congress-led central government dismissed the Punjab state government (led by their party), invoking the president's rule in the state.

During the five months before Operation Blue Star, from 1 January to 3 June 1984, 298 people were killed in violent incidents across Punjab. In the five days preceding the operation, 48 people were killed by violence. In the violent events leading up to the Operation Blue Star since the inception of Akali Dharm Yudh Morcha, the militants had killed 165 Hindus and Nirankaris, and even 39 Sikhs opposed to Bhindranwale were killed. The total number of deaths was 410 in violent incidents and riots while 1,180 people were injured.

On 1 June, Operation Blue Star was launched to remove him and the armed militants from the Golden Temple complex. On 6 June Bhindranwale died in the operation. Casualty figures for the Army were 83 dead and 249 injured. According to the official estimate presented by the Indian government, 1592 were apprehended and there were 493 combined militant and civilian casualties. High civilian casualties were attributed to militants using pilgrims trapped inside the temple as human shields. Later operations by Indian paramilitary forces were conducted to clear the separatists from the state of Punjab.

The operation carried out in the temple caused outrage among the Sikhs and increased the support for Khalistan Movement. Four months after the operation, on 31 October 1984, Indira Gandhi was assassinated in vengeance by her two Sikh bodyguards, Satwant Singh and Beant Singh. One of the assassins was fatally shot by Gandhi's other bodyguards while the other was convicted of Gandhi's murder and then executed. Public outcry over Gandhi's death led to the killings of Sikhs in the ensuing 1984 anti-Sikh riots.

After the assassination of Indira Gandhi on 31 October 1984 by two of her Sikh bodyguards, anti-Sikh riots erupted the following day. They continued in some areas for several days, killing more than 3,000 Sikhs in New Delhi and an estimated 8,000 – 17,000 or more Sikhs were killed in 40 cities across India. At least 50,000 Sikhs were displaced. Sultanpuri, Mangolpuri, Trilokpuri, and other Trans-Yamuna areas of Delhi were the worst affected.

Perpetrators carried iron rods, knives, clubs, and combustible material (including kerosene and petrol). They entered Sikh neighborhoods, killing Sikhs indiscriminately and destroying shops and houses. Armed mobs stopped buses and trains in and near Delhi, pulling off Sikh passengers for lynching; some were burnt alive. Others were dragged from their homes and hacked to death, and Sikh women were reportedly gang-raped and Sikhs also had acid thrown on them.

Such wide-scale violence cannot take place without police help. Delhi Police, whose paramount duty was to upkeep law and order situation and protect innocent lives, gave full help to rioters who were in fact working under able guidance of sycophant leaders like Jagdish Tytler and H K L Bhagat. It is a known fact that many jails, sub-jails and lock-ups were opened for three days and prisoners, for the most part hardened criminals, were provided fullest provisions, means and instruction to "teach the Sikhs a lesson". But it will be wrong to say that Delhi Police did nothing, for it took full and keen action against Sikhs who tried to defend themselves.

The Sikhs who opened fire to save their lives and property had to spend months dragging heels in courts after-wards. The riots have also been described as pogroms, massacres or genocide. On 31 October, a crowd around the All India Institute of Medical Sciences began shouting vengeance slogans such as "Blood for blood!" and became an unruly mob. At 17:20, President Zail Singh arrived at the hospital and the mob stoned his car. It began assaulting Sikhs, stopping cars and buses to pull Sikhs out and burn them.

The violence on 31 October, restricted to the area around the AIIMS, resulted in many Sikh deaths. Residents of other parts of Delhi reported that their neighborhoods were peaceful. During the night of 31 October and the morning of 1 November, Congress Party leaders met with local supporters to distribute money and weapons. Congress MP Sajjan Kumar and trade-union leader Lalit Maken handed out rupees 100 notes and bottles of liquor to the assailants. On the morning of 1 November, Sajjan Kumar was observed holding rallies in the Delhi neighborhoods of Palam Colony (from 06:30 to 07:00), Kiran Gardens (08:00 to 08:30), and Sultanpuri (about 08:30 to 09:00).

In Kiran Gardens at 8:00 am, Kumar was observed distributing iron rods from a parked truck to a group of 120 people and ordering them to "attack Sikhs, kill them, and loot and burn their properties". During the morning he led a mob along the Palam railway road to Mangolpuri, where the crowd chanted: "Kill the Sardars" and "Indira Gandhi is our mother and these people have killed her". In Sultanpuri, Moti Singh (a Sikh Congress Party member for 20 years) heard Kumar make the following speech:

Whoever kills the sons of the snakes, I will reward them. Whoever kills Roshan Singh and Bagh Singh will get 5,000 rupees each and 1,000 rupees each for killing any other Sikhs. You can collect these prizes on November 3 from my personal assistant Jai Chand Jamadar.

The Central Bureau of Investigation told the court that during the riot, Kumar said that "not a single Sikh should survive". The bureau accused Delhi police of keeping its "eyes closed" during the riot, which was planned.

In the Shakarpur neighborhood, Congress Party leader Shyam Tyagi's home was used as a meeting place for an undetermined number of people. Minister of Information and Broadcasting H. K. L. Bhagat gave money to Boop Tyagi (Tyagi's brother), saying: "Keep these two thousand rupees for liquor and do as I have told you ... You need not worry at all. I will look after everything."

During the night of 31 October, Balwan Khokhar (a local Congress Party leader who was implicated in the massacre) held a meeting at Pandit Harkesh's ration shop in Palam. Congress Party supporter Shankar Lal Sharma held a meeting, where he assembled a mob which swore to kill Sikhs, in his shop at 08:30 on 1 November.

Kerosene, the primary mob weapon, was supplied by a group of Congress Party leaders who owned filling stations. In Sultanpuri, Congress Party A-4 block president Brahmanand Gupta distributed oil while Sajjan Kumar "instructed the crowd to kill Sikhs, and to loot and burn their properties" (as he had done at other meetings throughout New Delhi). Similar meetings were held at locations such as Cooperative Colony in Bokaro, where local Congress president and gas-station owner P. K. Tripathi distributed kerosene to mobs.

Aseem Shrivastava, a graduate student at the Delhi School of Economics, described the mobs' organized nature in an affidavit submitted to the Misra Commission:

The attack on Sikhs and their property in our locality appeared to be an extremely organized affair ... There were also some young men on motorcycles, who were instructing the mobs and supplying them with kerosene oil from time to time. On more than a few occasions we saw auto-rickshaw arriving with several tins of kerosene oil and other inflammable material, such as jute sacks.

A senior official at the Ministry of Home Affairs told journalist Ivan Fera that an arson investigation of several businesses burned in the riots had found an unnamed combustible chemical "whose provision required large-scale coordination". Eyewitness reports confirmed the use of a combustible chemical in addition to kerosene.

The Delhi Sikh Gurdwara Management Committee later cited 70 affidavits noting the use of a highly-flammable chemical in its written reports to the Misra Commission.

On 31 October, Congress Party officials provided assailants with voter lists, school registration forms, and ration lists. The lists were used to find Sikh homes and business, an otherwise-impossible task because they were in unmarked, diverse neighborhoods. During the night of 31 October, before the massacres began, assailants used the lists to mark Sikh houses with an "S". Because most mob members were illiterate, Congress Party officials provided help reading the lists and leading the mobs to Sikh homes and businesses. With the lists, the mobs could pinpoint the location of Sikhs they otherwise would have missed.

Sikh men not at home were easily identified by their turbans and beards, and Sikh women were identified by their dress. In some cases, the mobs returned to locations where they knew Sikhs were hiding because of the lists. Amar Singh escaped the initial attack on his house by having a Hindu neighbor drag him into the neighbor's house and announce that he was dead.

A group of 18 assailants later came looking for his body; when his neighbor said that his body had been taken away, an assailant showed him a list and said: "Look, Amar Singh's name has not been struck off from the list, so his body has not been taken away."

The Delhi High Court, delivering its verdict on a riot-related case in 2009, said, "Though we boast of being the world's largest democracy and the Delhi being its national capital, the sheer mention of the incidents of 1984 anti-Sikh riots in general and the role played by Delhi Police and state machinery in particular makes our heads hang in shame in the eyes of the world polity."

The government allegedly destroyed evidence and shielded the guilty people involved in the massacre. The incident was criticized by some newspapers and radio channels, but not all. One of the newspapers of the capital, the Asian Age, an Indian daily newspaper, ran a front-page story calling the government actions "the mother of all cover-ups".

From 31 October 1984 to 10 November 1984 the People's Union for Democratic Rights and the People's Union for Civil Liberties conducted an inquiry into the riots, interviewing victims, police officers, neighbors of the victims, army personnel and political leaders. In their joint report, "Who Are The Guilty", the groups concluded:

The attacks on members of the Sikh Community in Delhi and its suburbs during the period, far from being a spontaneous expression of "madness" and of popular "grief and anger" at Mrs. Gandhi's assassination as made out to be by the authorities, were the outcome of a well-organized plan marked by acts of both deliberate commissions and omissions by important politicians of the Congress (I) at the top and by authorities in the administration.

According to eyewitness accounts obtained by Time magazine, Delhi police looked on as "rioters murdered and raped, having gotten access to voter records that allowed them to mark Sikh homes with large Xs, and large mobs being bused in to large Sikh settlements". Time reported that the riots led to only minor arrests, with no major politicians or police officers convicted. The magazine quoted Ensaaf, an Indian human-rights organization, as saying that the government attempted to destroy evidence of its involvement by refusing to record First Information Reports.

A 1991 Human Rights Watch report on violence between Sikh separatists and the Government of India traced part of the problem to government response to the violence:

Despite numerous credible eye-witness accounts that identified many of those involved in the violence, including police and politicians, in the months following the killings, the government sought no prosecutions or indictments of any persons, including officials, accused in any case of murder, rape or arson.

The violence was allegedly led (and often perpetrated) by Indian National Congress activists and sympathizers. The Congress-led government was widely criticized for doing little at the time and possibly conspiring in the riots, since voter lists were used to identify Sikh families.

A few days after the massacre, many surviving Sikh youths in Delhi had joined or created Sikh militant groups. This led to more violence in Punjab, including the assassination of several senior Congress Party members. The Khalistan Commando Force and Khalistan Liberation Force claimed responsibility for the retaliation, and an underground network was established.

On 31 July 1985, Harjinder Singh Jinda, Sukhdev Singh Sukha and Ranjit Singh Gill of the Khalistan Commando Force assassinated Congress Party leader and MP Lalit Maken in retaliation for the riots. The 31-page report, "Who Are The Guilty?" listed 227 people who led the mobs; Maken was third on the list.

Harjinder Singh Jinda and Sukhdev Singh Sukha assassinated Congress Party leader Arjan Dass because of his involvement in the riots. Dass' name appeared in affidavits submitted by Sikh victims to the Nanavati Commission, headed by retired Supreme Court of India judge G. T. Nanavati.

In Delhi, 442 rioters were convicted. Forty-nine were sentenced to the life imprisonment, and another three to more than 10 years' imprisonment. Six Delhi police officers were sanctioned for negligence during the riots. In April 2013, the Supreme Court of India dismissed the appeal of three people who had challenged their life sentences.

That month, the Karkardooma district court in Delhi convicted five people – Balwan Khokkar (former councilor), Mahender Yadav (former MLA), Kishan Khokkar, Girdhari Lal and Captain Bhagmal – for inciting a mob against Sikhs in Delhi Cantonment. The court acquitted Congress leader Sajjan Kumar, which led to protests.

In the first ever case of capital punishment in the 1984 anti-Sikh riots case death sentence was awarded to Yashpal Singh convicted for murdering two persons, 24-year-old Hardev Singh and 26-year-old Avtar Singh, in Mahipal Pur area of Delhi on 1 November 1984. Additional Sessions Judge Ajay Pandey pronounced the Judgment on 20 November 34 years after the crime was committed.

The second convict in the case, Naresh Sehrawat was awarded life imprisonment. The Court considered the failing health of 68-year-old Sehrawat while giving him a lighter sentence. The conviction followed a complaint by the deceased Hardev Singh's elder brother Santokh Singh.

Though an FIR was filed on the same day of the crime nothing came of the case as a Congress leader, JP Singh, who led the mob was acquitted in the case. A fresh FIR was filed on 29 April 1993, following recommendations of the Ranganath Commission of inquiry. The police closed the matter as untraced despite witness testimonies of the deceased's four brothers who were witness to the crime. The case was reopened by the Special Investigation Team constituted by the BJP-led NDA government on 12 February 2015.

The SIT completed the investigation in record time. The first conviction resulting from the formation of the SIT came on 15 November 2018, by the conviction of Naresh Sehrawat and Yashpal Singh. Subsequently, one of the first high-profile conviction of Sajjan Kumar by Delhi High Court who was earlier acquitted by the lower court on 17 December 2018.

Chapter 9

1989 insurgency in Kashmir
The Kashmir insurgency is an uprising or revolt against the Indian administration of Jammu and Kashmir, a region constituting the southern portion of the larger Kashmir region, which was the subject of a dispute between India and Pakistan since 1947.

Looking into the reason of uprising, we come to the fact that Jammu and Kashmir, long a breeding ground of separatist ambitions, has been wracked by the insurgency since 1989. Although the failure of Indian governance and democracy lay at the root of the initial disaffection, Pakistan played an important role in converting the latter into a fully developed insurgency.

Some insurgent groups in Kashmir support the complete independence, whereas others seek accession to Pakistan. More explicitly, the roots of the insurgency are tied to a dispute over local autonomy. Democratic development was limited in Kashmir until the late 1970s and by 1988 many of the democratic reforms provided by the Indian government had been reversed and non-violent channels for expressing discontent were limited and caused a dramatic increase in support for insurgents advocating violent secession from India.

In 1987, a disputed State election created a catalyst for the uprising when it resulted in some of the state's legislative assembly members forming armed rebellious groups. In July 1988, a series of demonstrations, strikes and attacks on the Indian government began the Kashmir insurgency, which during the 1990s escalated into the most important internal security issue in India.

Pakistan claims to be giving its "moral and diplomatic" support to the separatist movement. The Inter-Services Intelligence of Pakistan has been accused by India and the international community of supporting, supplying arms and training mujahideen, to fight in Jammu and Kashmir. In 2015, former President of Pakistan Pervez Musharraf admitted that Pakistan had supported and trained insurgent groups in the 1990s.

India has repeatedly called Pakistan to end its "cross-border terrorism" in Kashmir. Several new militant groups with radical Islamic views emerged and changed the ideological emphasis of the movement to Islamic. This had happened partly due to a large number of Islamic "Jihadi" fighters (mujahadeen) who had entered the Kashmir valley following the end of the Soviet–Afghan War in the 1980s.

The conflict between the militants and the Indian forces have led to large number of casualties. Many civilians have also died as a result of being targeted by the various armed groups. According to official figures released in Jammu and Kashmir assembly, there were 3,400 disappearance cases and the conflict has left more than 47,000 people dead which also includes 7,000 police personnel as of July 2009. However, the number of insurgency-related deaths in the state have fallen sharply since the start of a slow-moving peace process between India and Pakistan. Some rights groups claim a higher figure of 100,000 deaths since 1989.

After independence from colonial rule India and Pakistan fought a war over the princely state of Kashmir. At the end of the war India controlled the most valuable parts of Kashmir. While there were sporadic periods of violence there was no organized revolt movement. During this period legislative elections in Jammu and Kashmir were first held in 1951 and Sheikh Abdullah's secular party stood unopposed. He was an instrumental member in the accession of the state to India.

However Sheikh Abdullah would fall in and out of favor with the central government and would often be dismissed only to be re-appointed later on. This was a time of political instability & power struggle in Jammu and Kashmir and it went through several periods of President's rule by the Federal Government.

After Sheikh Abdullah's death, his son Farooq Abdullah took over as Chief Minister of Jammu and Kashmir. Farooq Abdullah eventually fell out of favor with the Central Government and the Prime Minister Indira Gandhi had his government toppled with the help of his brother-in-law G. M. Shah. A year later, Abdullah reached an accord with the new Prime Minister Rajiv Gandhi and announced an alliance with the Congress party for the elections of 1987. The elections were allegedly rigged in favor of Abdullah.

Most commentators state that this led to the rise of an armed insurgency movement composed, in part, of those who unfairly lost the elections. Pakistan supplied these groups with logistical support, arms, recruits and training.

In the second half of 1989 the alleged assassinations of the Indian spies and political collaborators by JKLF (Jammu and Kashmir Liberation Front) was intensified. Over six months, more than a hundred officials were killed to paralyses government's administrative and intelligence apparatus.

The daughter of then interior affairs minister, Mufti Mohammad Sayeed was kidnapped in December and four terrorists had to be released for her release. This event led to mass celebrations all over the valley. Farooq Abdullah resigned in January after the appointment of Jagmohan Malhotra as the Governor of Jammu and Kashmir. Subsequently, J&K was placed under Governor's Rule under Article 92 of state constitution.

Under JKLF's leadership on January 21–23 large scale protests were organized in valley. As a response to this largely explosive situation paramilitary units of BSF and CRPF were called. These units were used by the government to combat Maoist and North-Eastern rebellions.

The challenge to them in this situation was not posed by armed insurgents but by the stone palters. Their inexperience caused at least 50 casualties in Gawkadal massacre. In this incident the underground militant movement was transformed into a mass struggle. To curb the situation AFSPA (Armed Forces Special Powers Act) was imposed on Kashmir in September 1990 to suppress the radical movement by giving armed forces the powers to kill and arrest without warrant to maintain public order.

During this time the dominant tactic involved killing of a prominent figure in a public gathering to push forces into action and the public prevented them from capturing these insurgents. This sprouting of sympathizers in Kashmir led to the hardline approach of Indian army.

With JKLF at forefront large number of militant groups like Allah Tigers, People's League and Hizb-i-Islamia sprung up. Weapons were smuggled on a large scale from Pakistan. In Kashmir, JKLF operated under the leadership of Ashfaq Majid Wani, Yasin Bhat, Hamid Shiekh and Javed Mir.

To counter this growing pro-Pakistani sentiment in the Kashmir region, Indian media associated it exclusively with Pakistan. JKLF militant force used distinctly Islamic themes to mobilize crowds and justify their use of violence. They sought to establish an Islamic democratic state where the rights of minorities would be protected according to Quran and Sunna and economy would be organized on the principles of Islamic socialism.

The Indian army has conducted various operations to control and eliminate insurgency in the region such as Operation Sarp Vinash, in which a multi-battalion offensive was launched against terrorists from groups like Lashkar-e-Taiba, Harkat-ul-Jihad-e-Islami, al-Badr and Jaish-e-Mohammad who had been constructing shelters in the Pir Panjal region of Jammu and Kashmir over several years.

The subsequent operations led to the death of over 60 terrorists and uncovered the largest network of militant hideouts in the history of Jammu and Kashmir covering 100 square kilometers. During the early period of militancy in 1989, multiple militants groups strive to Islamize Kashmiri culture and political setup to create a conducive environment for the merger of Kashmir with Pakistan. Numerous Islamist groups were formed in early 1990 who emerged advocating Nizam-e-Mustafa (Rule of Muhammad) as the objective for their struggle.

Militant groups like Hizbul mujahideen and Jamaat-e-Islami asserted that struggle of Kashmir will continue till Islamic Caliphate is achieved in Kashmir. Murder of Kashmiri Hindus, Intellectuals, Liberals and activists were described necessary to get rid of un-Islamic elements.

Concurrently all cinema houses, beauty parlors, wine shops, dance bars, video centers, use of cosmetics and similar things were banned by militant groups. Many militant organizations like Al baqr, People's league, Wahdat-e-Islam and Allah Tigers imposed restrictions like banning cigarettes, restrictions on Kashmiri girls.

Apart from militants, Kashmir was witnessing Islamization during 1980's when Abdullah Government changed the names of about 2,500 villages from their native names to new Islamic names. The Sheikh also started delivering communal speeches in mosques similar to his speeches in the 1930s. Additionally, he referred Kashmiri Pandits as "mukhbir" or informers of the Indian government.

The Afghan jihad against the Soviets, the Islamic Revolution in Iran, and the armed struggle of the Sikhs in Punjab against the Indian state became sources of inspiration for large numbers of Kashmiri Muslim youth. Both the pro-Independence JKLF and the pro-Pakistan Islamist groups including Jamaat-e-Islami Kashmir mobilized the fast growing anti-Indian sentiments among the Kashmiri population. The year of 1984 saw a pronounced rise in terrorist violence in Kashmir. When the JKLF militant Maqbool Bhat was executed in February 1984, strikes and protests by Kashmiri nationalists broke out in the region, where large number of Kashmiri youth participated in widespread anti-India demonstrations, which faced heavy handed reprisals by the state forces.

The Hindus of the Kashmir Valley, were forced to flee the Kashmir valley as a result of being targeted by JKLF and Islamist insurgents during late 1989 and early 1990. Of the approximately 300,000 to 600,000 Hindus living in the Kashmir Valley in 1990 only 2,000–3,000 remain there in 2016.

January 19, 1990 is widely remembered by Kashmiri Hindus as the tragic "exodus day" of being forced out of Kashmir. According to the Indian government, more than 62,000 families are registered as Kashmiri refugees including some Sikh and Muslim families. Most families were resettled in Jammu, National Capital Region surrounding Delhi and other neighboring states.

Under the 1975 accord, Sheikh Abdullah agreed to measures previously undertaken by the central government in Jammu and Kashmir to integrate the state into India. Sociologist Farrukh Faheem states that it was met with hostility among people of Kashmir and laid the groundwork for the future uproar in the state.

Those opposed to it included Jamaat-e-Islami Kashmir and People's League in Indian Jammu and Kashmir, and Jammu Kashmir Liberation Front (JKLF) based in Azad Kashmir. Since the mid-1970s, communalist rhetoric was being exploited in the state for vote-bank politics. Pakistan's Inter-Services Intelligence (ISI) tried to spread Wahhabism in place of Sufism to foster religious unity with their nation, the communalization helped in furthering it.

February 1986, Gul Shah on his return to Kashmir valley retaliated and incited the Kashmiri Muslims by saying Islam is in danger. As a result, Kashmiri Hindus were targeted by the Kashmiri Muslims. Many incidents were reported in various areas where Kashmiri Hindus were killed and their properties and temples damaged or destroyed. The worst hit areas were mainly in South Kashmir.

During the Anantnag riot in February 1986, although no Hindu was killed, many houses and other properties belonging to Hindus were looted, burnt or damaged. An investigation of Anantnag riots revealed that members of the 'secular parties' in the state, rather than the Islamists, had played a key role in organizing the violence to gain political mileage through religious sentiments. Shah called in the army to curb the violence, but it had little effect. His government was dismissed on 12 March 1986, by the then Governor Jagmohan following communal riots in south Kashmir.

This led Jagmohan to rule the state directly. The political fight was hence being portrayed as a conflict between "Hindu" New Delhi (Central Government), and its efforts to impose its will in the state, and "Muslim" Kashmir, represented by political Islamists and clerics. Islamists had organized under a banner named Muslim United Front, with manifesto to work for Islamic unity and against political interference from the center, and contested the 1987 state elections, in which they lost again.

However, the 1987 elections were widely believed to be rigged so as to bring the secular parties in Kashmir at the forefront, and this caused the insurgency in Kashmir. The Kashmiri militants killed anyone who openly expressed pro-India policies. Kashmiri Hindus were targeted specifically because they were seen as presenting Indian presence in Kashmir because of their faith.

Though the insurgency had been launched by JKLF, groups rose over the next few months advocating for establishment of Nizam-e-Mustafa (Rule of Muhammad). The Islamist groups proclaimed the Islamicization of socio-political and economic set-up, merger with Pakistan, unification of ummah and establishment of an Islamic Caliphate.

Liquidation of central government officials, Hindus, liberal and nationalist intellectuals, social and cultural activists was described as necessary to rid the valley of un-Islamic elements. The relations among the semi-secular and Islamists groups were generally poor and often hostile. The JKLF had also utilized Islamic formulations in its mobilization strategies and public discourse, using Islam and independence interchangeably. It demanded equal rights for everyone however this had a distinct Islamic flavor as it sought to establish an Islamic democracy, protection of minority rights per Quran and Sunnah and an economy of Islamic socialism. The pro-separatist political practices at times deviated from their stated secular position.

The JKLF group targeted a Kashmiri Hindu for the first time on 14 September 1989, when they killed Tika Lal Taploo, an advocate and a prominent leader of Bharatiya Janata Party in Jammu & Kashmir in front of several eyewitnesses. This instilled fear in the Kashmiri Hindus especially as Taploo's killers were never caught which also emboldened the terrorists.

The Hindus felt that they weren't safe in the valley and could be targeted any time. The killings of Kashmiri Hindus continued that included many of the prominent ones. In order to undermine his political rival, Farooq Abdullah who at that time was the Chief Minister of Jammu and Kashmir, the Minister of Home Affairs Mufti Mohammad Sayeed convinced Prime Minister V.P. Singh to appoint Jagmohan as the governor of the state.

Abdullah resented Jagmohan who had been appointed as the governor earlier in April 1984 as well and had recommended Abdullah's dismissal to Rajiv Gandhi in July 1984. Abdullah had earlier declared that he would resign if Jagmohan was made the Governor. However, the Central government went ahead and appointed him as Governor on 19 January 1990. In response, Abdullah resigned on the same day and Jagmohan suggested the dissolution of the State Assembly.

Chapter 10

Ayodhya firing incident

Uttar Pradesh state of India started facing turbulence since 1990. The center of Hindu uprising was the Ram Janmabhoomi of Ayodhya. The Ayodhya firing incident describes the occasion when the Uttar Pradesh police fired live ammunition at civilians on two separate days, 30 October 1990 and 2 November 1990. The civilians were religious Hindu volunteers, assembled near the Ram Janmabhoomi site at Ayodhya. The state government's official records report that 16 people were killed.

In September 1990, the Vishwa Hindu Parishad (VHP), the Rashtriya Swayamsevak Sangh (RSS) and the Bhartiya Janata Party campaigned for a new Ram Temple to be built at the Ram Janmabhoomi site. The situation became volatile, with L. K. Advani conducting rath yatra and the VHP mobilizing people to the site. The state government, under Mulayam Singh Yadav, promised protection and a complete lockdown of the site and city. Yadav reassured the public: "No bird would be able to fly into Ayodhya".

The Hindu volunteers first assembled in Ayodhya, at the behest of L. K. Advani of the BJP and Ashok Singhal of the VHP, on 21 October 1990. Just two weeks later, 30 October saw the start of unprecedented security arrangements in the state. Police barred all bus and train services to Ayodhya. Most volunteers reached Ayodhya by foot; some swam across the Sarayu River.

The police also barricaded the 1.5 km-long climb to the disputed structure and imposed a curfew. According to the investigatory Liberhan Commission report, issued after the event:

28,000 Uttar Pradesh Provincial Armed Constabulary personnel were deployed in Ayodhya.
Out of 40,000 volunteers, only 10,000 managed to reach Ayodhya.
At around 10 am, a large group of volunteers headed towards the site.

The large group was led by Vamadev, Mahant Nratyagopal Das, and Ashok Singhal of the VHP. Ashok Singhal was wounded on the head by a police baton. This altercation led to a mob frenzy and open confrontation between civilians and policemen. At around 11 am, a Hindu holy-man or sadhu managed to gain control of an Armed Constabulary bus in which the police were holding detainees. The sadhu drove the bus right through the barricades, clearing a way for the others to follow on foot. The security forces were caught off guard and were forced to chase about 5,000 volunteers, who stormed through the heavily guarded site.

According to eyewitnesses the Kothari brothers mounted a saffron flag atop the Babri Masjid. On the orders of Mulayam Government, security personnel fired on the crowd and chased volunteers across the area. Many people died from head wounds. There was a stampede at the Saryu Bridge, which killed a number of people.

Hindu groups took a day of rest on 1 November. On 2 November 1990, they offered prayers at Ramlila in the morning and then proceeded to Babri Masjid. Members of the crowd used the strategy of touching security personnel's feet, which made them withdraw a step. This worked for a while, and the procession continued. However, the police took firm action by using tear gas and baton charges to disperse the crowd. Nevertheless, some contingents of volunteers reached and partially damaged the mosque.

In response, the police opened fire for the second time in 72 hours, and chased them through the alleys around Hanumangarhi. In one place, later named Shaheed Gali or Martyr's Alley, police killed many of them – this included the Kothari Brothers, who were allegedly dragged out of a mosque.

Some liberal Indians have accused the police of disposing of many dead bodies, either by cremating them at unknown places or by dumping them into the Saryu River in sacks. News of the shootings was mostly suppressed from the Indian media, but some local and international media outlets mentioned them on their channels.

The firing incident had a major impact on Uttar Pradesh and on Indian national politics. The Chief Minister of Uttar Pradesh was given the sobriquet 'Mulla' Mulayam Singh for his pro-Muslim stance during the incident. He lost the 1991 election to the Bhartiya Janata Party. He described his decision to fire on the crowd in Ayodhya as "painful yet necessary as it was ordered by the high court to maintain peace, law and order till the judgment come out."

People of the Hindu community arranged a memorial meeting for the dead volunteers on April 4, 1991 at the Boat Club, New Delhi, which attracted a large audience. They explained in detail about the happening. They also launched a nationwide awareness program displaying the Asthi Kalash (funeral urns) of those who died in the firing incident. In the following years, these organizations and their prominent leaders received both political and moral endorsement. And, on 6 December 1992, a large group volunteers completely demolished Babri Masjid.

Chapter 11

1992 Bombay riots

The Bombay riots usually refers to the riots in Mumbai, during two months, December 1992 and January 1993. It took the life of approximately 900 people in Mumbai. The riots were mainly due to the escalations of hostilities after large scale protests by Muslims in reaction to the 1992 Babri Masjid Demolition by Hindu volunteers in Ayodhya.

The violence was widely reported as having been orchestrated by the Shiv Sena, a Hindu-nationalist political party in Maharashtra. A high-ranking member of the special branch later stated that the police were fully aware of the Shiv Sena's capabilities to commit acts of violence, and that they had incited hate against the minority communities.

Historian Barbara Metcalf has stated that the riots were anti-Muslim pogrom. The riots were followed by the retaliatory 12 March 1993 Bombay Bombings. The Bombay riots can be considered a result of larger communal tensions throughout India. The British colonial policy of Divide and Rule allegedly included administrative and political activities such as communalized census taking, and the Morley Minto reforms, that relied on communal segregation, and in particular Hindu-Muslim divisions.

Post-Independence, the after-effects of the Partition of India along communal lines, the resurgence of 'Hindu Muslim Economic competition', the growth of right-wing communalist movements such as the RSS, and political strategies of 'appeasement' towards communal political influences by secular political authorities, reinforced communalist ideologies in the country. The Babri Mosque demolition on 6 December 1992, an act of communal violence by Hindu extremist, is considered to be the immediate cause of the riots.

As determined by the government's Srikrishna commission; the riots started as a result of communal tension prevailing in the city after the Babri Mosque demolition on 6 December 1992. The Commission identified two phases to the riots. The first was mainly a Muslim instigation as a result of the Babri Masjid demolition in the week immediately succeeding 7 December 1992 led by political leaders representing Hindutva in the city of Ayodhya.

The second phase was a Hindu backlash occurring as a result of the killings of Hindu Mathadi Kamgar (workers) by Muslim fanatics in Dongri, an area of South Bombay, stabbing of Hindus in Muslim majority areas and burning of six Hindus, including a disabled girl in Radhabai Chawl. This phase occurred in January 1993, with most incidents reported between 6 and 20 January.

The Report asserted that the communal passions of the Hindus were aroused to fever pitch by the inciting writings in print media, particularly Saamna and Navaakal which gave exaggerated accounts of the Mathadi murders and the Radhabai Chawl incident. From 8 January 1993, many riots occurred between Hindus led by the Shiv Sena and Muslims potentially funded by the Bombay underworld at that time.

An estimated 575 Muslims and 275 Hindus were killed at the end of the riot. The communal violence and rioting triggered off by the burning at Dongri and Radhabhai Chawl, and the following retaliatory violence by Shiv Sena was hijacked by local criminal elements whose potential opportunity was to make quick gains. By the time the right wing Hindu organization, Shiv Sena realized that enough had been done by way of "retaliation", the violence and rioting was beyond the control of its leaders who had to issue an appeal to put an end to it.

News of the demolition of Babri Masjid spread by 14:30 hours on 6 December 1992. Muslims angered by this act felt that Islam was in imminent danger since proponents of the Hindu nation had been allowed to destroy, under the very nose of the police forces, the Babri Masjid, despite assurances and undertakings by the Uttar Pradesh state Government and the Government of India that no harm would be permitted to be caused to the Babri Masjid.

The extensive media coverage, particularly on television, of footage of file pictures of Hindus dancing on the dome of the Masjid, as well as the latest video shots showing actual demolition of the Babri Masjid, caused a sense of deep resentment. The demolition of the Babri Masjid provided enough fuel to excite, ignite and exploit the sentimentalities of the Indian Muslims. Muslims were proselytized by these exploitative elements that the Establishment and the Government had an active hand in the destruction, since it did not do anything to prevent the same.

Rumors abounded that alleged members of certain Hindutva parties were seen to be celebrating the demolition of Babri structure. Muslims protested violently on the streets. A large number of Muslims congregated near Minara Masjid in Pydhonie jurisdiction in South Mumbai at about 23:20 hours on 6 December 1992 and came out protesting frenziedly. The first targets of the rioting mob became the municipal vans and the constabulary, both visible signs of the government.

Activists of Bharatiya Janata Party and Shiv Sena jumped into the fray, and escalated communal sentiments, as seen from their act of stopping the vehicles on roads in the jurisdiction of V.P. Road Police Station. In Nirmal Nagar jurisdiction, a Ganesh idol in the Ganesh Mandir on Anant Kanekar Marg was found moved out from its place of installation though the lock on the grill surrounding the sanctum was found intact. This was noticed at about 23:45 hours.

At the time the incident happened, there were no immediate clues as to the identity of the miscreants. It was widely rumored that Muslim fanatics were behind it. Following the rumor, in the jurisdiction of Deonar, there was a sharp counter—reaction by Muslims who stoned the house of a local Bharatiya Janata Party leader.

Two constables in Deonar jurisdiction were killed with choppers and swords by the rampaging Muslims, while one lay on the ground bleeding to death, the body of another was dragged and thrown into the garbage heap from where it was recovered seven days later. One constable was done to death in Byculla jurisdiction. Several police officers and policemen who bravely attempted to stem the tide sustained injuries in mob action.

Jogeshwari area, which has been the hotbed of frequent communal riots, saw serious riots at the junction of Pascal Colony and Shankar Wadi. A police officer on duty received a bullet injury in his head and died subsequently, though it cannot be said with certitude that it was a case of private firing. The police recovered large number of iron rods, sickles, choppers, knives and soda water bottles from different jurisdictions indicating that there was intention and preparations to carry on the communal riots.

A violent Muslim mob ransacked a Police station at Maulana Shaukat Ali Road and physically assaulted one Police constable, Pandit Malhari Ahire. Ahire was attacked with swords and choppers and suffered grievous injuries. At about the same time a huge Muslim mob of about 4,000–5,000 collected on Maulana Shaukat Ali Road and in the lanes and by–lanes of the area. The mob went on damaging and destroying the vehicles and public property and indulged in throwing stones.

Ahire's life was saved by prompt action by Senior Police Inspector Pawar along with other officers who carried on firing to restore peace. On 8 December 1992 communal rioting and communal violence spread to 33 jurisdictions, the number of clashes of rioting mobs with police as well as rioting mobs increased alarmingly. Attacks on places of worship also continued. Shiv Sena systematically attacked Muslim men, women and children during that time.

The police had to resort to firing in 43 cases resulting in the death of 11 Hindus, 31 Muslims and three others. There were several cases of mob violence, stabbing and arson. One temple in Dharavi, one in Deonar, one in Park Site and one in Saki Naka were attacked. Simultaneously, two mosques in Dharavi, one madrasa in Mahim and Bhoiwada each and one dargah in Dadar was also attacked.

Though the police found their resources stretched, they were unwilling to take the help of army for carrying out operational duties. Army columns were used only to carry out flag marches which had little impact on the, by now hardened and emboldened, rioters. The imposition of curfew from the night of 7 December 1992 also did not appear to deter the clashing mobs in view of its effete enforcement. Police intervention came about by resort to fire on 72 occasions, killing 15 Hindus and 72 Muslims and injuring 131 Muslims and one Christian.

By the 10th December, the situation had improved further with the number of police stations affected coming down to four, though serious communal riots occurred in Dharavi and Mahim,police jurisdictions to control, and the police had to fire on three and two occasions respectively.

By the 12th December, the situation showed further enhancement and the number of police stations affected came down to 14, though there also the occurrences were stray. There were three instances of police firing, one each in Ghatkopar, Bhandup and Dindoshi. Mob violence took the toll of one life. There were six cases of stabbing. There were eight stray cases of arson. Four dead bodies, all of Muslims, having multiple stab wounds on vital organs and in highly decomposed condition, were recovered from a gutter in Golibar area.

However, beneath the surface there was simmering discontent and seething anger amongst the Muslims that unduly excessive police firing had resulted in large number of Muslim casualties. Media had criticized the police for having used unnecessary and excessive fire–power, going so far as to suggest that Muslims were intentionally targeted and selectively killed. This refrain was repeated by political leaders and ministers, past and current.

The explanation of the commissioner of police that the aggressive and violent mobs in the initial stages comprised Muslims and therefore, Muslim casualties were higher. Considering it from all aspects, the Commission was not inclined to give serious credence to the theory that dis–proportionately large number of Muslim deaths in December 1992 was necessarily indicative of an attempt on the part of the police to target and liquidate Muslims because of bias.

On 20 December 1992, two Muslims were locked inside a room in Goregaon, and the room was set on fire as a result of which they suffered severe burns resulting in the death of one. Two bodies, one of a male Hindu and another identified as that of a uniformed Muslim police constable attached to the Nasik Rural Police Headquarters, were recovered from the septic tank of the public latrine in Behrampada on 20 and 21 December 1992 respectively. These bodies bore multiple stab injuries. It would appear that there was a systematic attempt to stab and murder Hindus and the policeman.

From 20 January 1993 onwards there was no major communal incident despite a few stray cases being reported. A call was given out by Imam of Jama Masjid that Muslims should boycott the Republic Day and hoist black flags on their establishments and houses. Police maintained continued vigil along with the army and paramilitary forces.

During the subsequent period in January, the situation in the city slowly comes back to normalcy. The total number of deaths was 900. The causes for the deaths are police firing (356), stabbing (347), arson (91), mob action (80), private firing (22) and other causes (4).

The violence was widely reported as having been orchestrated by the Shiv Sena, a Hindu-nationalist political party in Maharashtra. A high-ranking member of the special branch later stated that the police were fully aware of the Shiv Sena's capabilities to commit acts of violence, and that they had incited hate against the minority communities. Historian Barbara Metcalf has stated that the riots were anti-Muslim pogrom.

Bal Thackeray, the then-leader of the Shiv Sena, was arrested in July 2000 for his complicity in the riots and for 'inflammatory writings' that may have helped propagate the riots. But the case went loose, and it was later dismissed.

Justice Srikrishna, then a relatively junior Judge of the Bombay High Court, accepted the task of investigating the causes of the riots, something that many of his colleagues had turned down. For five years until 1998, he examined victims, witnesses and alleged perpetrators. Detractors came initially from left quarters who were wary of a judge who was a devout and practicing Hindu. The Commission was disbanded by the Shiv Sena led government in January 1996 and on public opposition was later reconstituted on 28 May 1996; though when it was reconstituted, its terms of reference were extended to include the Bombay bomb blasts that followed in March 1993.

The report of the commission stated that the tolerant and secular foundations of the city were holding even if a little shakily. Justice Srikrishna indicted those he alleged as largely responsible for the second phase of the bloodshed and to some extent the first, the Shiv Sena.

The report was criticized as "politically motivated". For a while, its contents were a closely guarded secret and no copies were available. The Shiv Sena government rejected its recommendations. Since under the Commissions of Inquiry Act, an Inquiry is not a court of law (even if it conducts proceedings like a court of law) and the report of an inquiry is not binding on Governments, Srikrishna's recommendations cannot be directly enforced.

To date, the recommendations of the Commission have neither been accepted nor acted upon by the Maharashtra Government. Many indicted policemen were promoted by the government and indicted politicians continue to hold high political office even today. Only 3 convictions happened in the 1992-93 Bombay riots cases. On 10 July 2008, a Mumbai court sentenced former Shiv Sena MP Madhukar Sarpotdar and two other party activists to a year's rigorous imprisonment in connection with the riots.[17][18] However, he was immediately granted bail.

Chapter 12

2002 Gujarat riots

The 2002 Gujarat riots was a three-day period of inter-communal violence in the western Indian state of Gujarat. Following the initial incident, there were further outbreaks of violence in Ahmedabad for three months; statewide, there were further outbreaks of violence against the minority Muslim population for the next year. The burning of a train in Godhra on 27 February 2002, which caused the deaths of 58 Hindu pilgrims returning from Ayodhya, is cited as having instigated the violence.

According to official figures already published, the riots ended with 1,044 dead, 223 missing, and 2,500 injured. Of the dead, 790 were Muslim and 254 Hindu. The Concerned Citizens Tribunal Report, estimated that as many as 1,926 may have been killed. Other sources estimated death tolls in excess of 2,000 people of the state.

Many brutal killings and rapes were reported on as well as widespread looting and destruction of property. Narendra Modi, then Chief Minister of Gujarat and later Prime Minister of India, was accused of initiating and condoning the violence, as were police and government officials who allegedly directed the rioters and gave lists of Muslim-owned properties to them.

In March month of 2012, Narendra Modi was cleared of complicity in the violence by Special Investigation Team (SIT) appointed by the Supreme Court of India. The SIT also rejected claims that the state government had not done enough to prevent the riots. Muslim community was reported to have reacted with anger and disbelief.

In July 2013, allegations were made that the SIT had suppressed evidence. That December, an Indian court upheld the earlier SIT report and rejected a petition seeking Modi's prosecution. In April 2014, the Supreme Court expressed satisfaction over the SIT's investigations in nine cases related to the violence, and rejected a plea contesting the SIT report as "baseless".

Though officially classified as a communalist riot, the events of 2002 have been described as a pogrom by many scholars, with some commentators alleging that the attacks had been planned, with the attack on the train was a "staged trigger" for what was actually premeditated violence. Other observers have stated that these events had met the "legal definition of genocide," or referred to them as state terrorism or ethnic cleansing.

Instances of mass violence include the Naroda Patiya massacre that took place directly adjacent to a police training camp; the Gulbarg Society massacre where Ehsan Jafri, a former parliamentarian was among those killed; and several incidents in Vadodara city. Scholars studying the 2002 riots state that they were premeditated and constituted a form of ethnic cleansing, and that the state government and law enforcement were complicit in the violence that occurred.

On the morning of 27 February 2002, the Sabarmati Express, returning from Ayodhya to Ahmedabad, stopped near the Godhra railway station. The passengers were Hindu pilgrims, returning from Ayodhya after a religious ceremony at the site of the demolished Babri Masjid. An argument erupted between the train passengers and the vendors on the railway platform. The argument became violent and under uncertain circumstances four coaches of the train caught fire with many people trapped inside.

In the resulting conflagration, 59 people (nine men, 25 women, and 25 children) burned to death. The government of Gujarat set up Gujarat High Court judge K. G. Shah as a one-man commission to look into the incident, but following outrage among families of victims and in the media over Shah's alleged closeness to Modi, retired Supreme Court judge G.T. Nanavati was added as chairman of the now two-person commission.

After six years of going over the details, the commission submitted its preliminary report which concluded that the fire was an act of arson, committed by a mob of one to two thousand locals. Maulvi Husain Haji Ibrahim Umarji, a cleric in Godhra, and a dismissed Central Reserve Police Force officer named Nanumiyan were presented as the "masterminds" behind the arson. After 24 extensions, the commission submitted its final report on 18 November 2014.

The findings of the commission were called into question by a video recording released by Tehelka magazine, which showed Arvind Pandya, counsel for the Gujarat government, stating that the findings of the Shah-Nanavati commission would support the view presented by the Bharatiya Janata Party (BJP), as Shah was "their man" and Nanavati could be bribed.

In February 2011, the trial court convicted 31 people and acquitted 63 others based on the murder and conspiracy provisions of the Indian Penal Code, saying the incident was a "pre-planned conspiracy." Of those convicted, 11 were sentenced to death and the other 20 to life in prison. Maulvi Umarji, presented by the Nanavati-Shah commission as the prime conspirator, was acquitted along with 62 others accused for lack of evidence.

The Union government led by the Indian National Congress party in 2005 also set up a committee to probe the incident, headed up by retired Supreme Court judge Umesh Chandra Banerjee. The committee concluded that the fire had begun inside the train and was most likely accidental. However, the Gujarat High Court ruled in 2006 that the matter was outside the jurisdiction of the union government, and that the committee was therefore unconstitutional.

The Concerned Citizens Tribunal (CCT) concluded that the fire had been an accident. Several other independent commentators have also concluded that the fire itself was almost certainly an accident, saying that the initial cause of the conflagration has never been conclusively determined. Historian Ainslie Thomas Embree stated that the official story of the attack on the train (that it was organized and carried out by people under orders from Pakistan) was entirely baseless.

Following the attack on the train, the Vishva Hindu Parishad (VHP) called for a statewide strike. Although the Supreme Court had declared such strikes to be unconstitutional and illegal, and despite the common tendency for such strikes to be followed by violence, no action was taken by the state to prevent the strike.

The government did not attempt to stop the initial outbreak of violence across the state. Independent reports indicate that the state BJP president Rana Rajendrasinh had endorsed the strike, and that Modi and Rana used inflammatory language which worsened the situation.

Then-Chief Minister Narendra Modi declared that the attack on the train had been an act of terrorism, and not an incident of communal violence. Local newspapers and members of the state government used the statement to incite violence against the Muslim community by claiming, without proof that the attack on the train was carried out by Pakistan's intelligence agency and that local Muslims had conspired with them to attack Hindus in the state.

False stories were also printed by local newspapers which claimed that Muslim people had kidnapped and raped Hindu women. Numerous accounts describe the attacks on the Muslim community that began on 28 February (the day after the train fire) as highly coordinated with mobile phones and government-issued printouts listing the homes and businesses of Muslims. Attackers arrived in Muslim communities across the region in trucks, wearing saffron robes and khaki shorts (the unofficial uniform of Hindu nationalism) and bearing a variety of weapons.

In many cases, attackers damaged or burned Muslim-owned or occupied buildings while leaving adjacent Hindu buildings untouched. Although many calls to the police were made from victims, they were told by the police that "we have no orders to save you." In some cases, the police fired on Muslims who attempted to defend themselves. The rioters used mobile phones to coordinate their attacks.

By the end of the day on 28 February a curfew had been declared in 27 towns and cities across the state. A government minister stated that although the circumstances were tense in Baroda and Ahmedabad, the situation was under control, and that the police who had been deployed were enough to prevent any violence. In Baroda the administration imposed a curfew in seven areas of the city.

M. D. Antani, then the deputy superintendent of police, deployed the Rapid Action Force to sensitive areas in Godhra. Gordhan Zadafia, the Minister of State for Home, believed there would be no retaliation from the Hindu community for the train burning. Modi stated that the violence was no longer as intense as it had been and that it would soon be brought under control, and that if the situation warranted it, the police would be supported by deploying the army. A shoot-to-kill order was issued, however, the troop deployment was withheld by the state government until 1 March, when the most severe violence had ended. After more than two months of violence a unanimous vote to authorize central intervention was passed in the upper house of parliament.

Members of the opposition made accusations that the government had failed to protect Muslim people in the worst rioting in India in more than 10 years. It is estimated that 230 mosques and 274 dargahs were destroyed during the violence. For the first time in the history of communal riots Hindu women took part, looting Muslim shops. It is estimated that up to 150,000 people were displaced during the violence. It is estimated that 200 police officers died while trying to control the violence, and Human Rights Watch reported that acts of exceptional heroism were committed by Hindus, Dalits and tribals who tried to protect Muslims from the violence.

In the aftermath of the violence, it became clear that many attacks were focused not only on Muslim populations, but also on Muslim women and children. Organizations such as Human Rights Watch criticized the Indian government and the Gujarat state administration for failure to address the resulting humanitarian condition of victims who fled their homes for relief camps during the violence, the "overwhelming majority of them Muslim."

According to Teesta Setalvad on 28 February in the districts of Morjari Chowk and Charodia Chowk in Ahmedabad of all forty people who had been killed by police shooting were Muslim. An international fact-finding committee formed of all women international experts from US, UK, France, Germany and Sri Lanka reported, "sexual violence was being used as a strategy for terrorizing women belonging to minority community in the state."

It is estimated that at least two-hundred and fifty girls and women were gang raped and then burned to death. Children were force fed petrol and then set on fire, pregnant women were gutted and then had their unborn child's body shown to them. In the Naroda Patiya mass grave of ninety-six bodies, forty-six were women.

Rioters also flooded homes and electrocuted entire families inside. Violence against women also included them being stripped naked, violated with objects, and then killed. According to Kalpana Kannabiran the rapes were part of a well-organized, deliberate and pre-planned strategy, and which facts place the violence into the categories of political pogrom and genocide. Other acts of violence against women included acid attacks, beatings and the killing of women who were pregnant.

Children were also killed in front of their parents. George Fernandes in a discussion in parliament on the violence caused widespread furor in his defense of the state government, said that this was not the first time that women had been violated and raped in India.

Children were killed by being burnt alive and those who dug the mass graves described the bodies interred within them as "burned and butchered beyond recognition." Children and infants were speared and held aloft before being thrown into fires. Describing the sexual violence perpetrated against Muslim women and girls, Renu Khanna writes that the survivors reported that it "consisted of forced nudity, mass rapes, gang-rapes, mutilation, insertion of objects into bodies, cutting of breasts, slitting the stomach and reproductive organs, and carving of Hindu religious symbols on women's body parts."

Barring a few, in most instances of sexual violence, the women victims were stripped and paraded naked, then gang-raped, and thereafter quartered and burnt beyond recognition. The leaders of the mobs even raped young girls, some as young as 11 years old, before burning them alive. Even a 20-day-old infant, or a fetus in the womb of its mother, was not spared.

Vandana Shiva stated that "Young boys have been taught to burn, rape and kill in the name of Hindutva." Dionne Bunsha, writing on the Gulbarg Society massacre and murder of Ehsan Jafri, has said that when Jafri begged the crowd to spare the women, he was dragged into the street and forced to parade naked for refusing to say "Jai Shri Ram." He was then beheaded and thrown onto a fire, after which rioters returned and burned Jafri's family, including two small boys, to death. After the massacre Gulbarg remained in flames for a week.

The Times of India reported that over ten thousand Hindus were displaced during the violence. According to police records, 157 riots after the Godhra incident were started by Muslims. In Mahajan No Vando, a Hindu residential area in Jamalpur, residents reported that Muslim attackers injured approximately twenty-five Hindu residents and destroyed five houses on 1 March. The community head reported that the police responded quickly, but were ineffectual as there were so few of them present to help during the attack. The colony was later visited by Modi on 6 March, who promised the residents that they would be taken care of.

On 17 March, it was reported that Muslims attacked Dalits in the Danilimda area of Ahmedabad. In Himatnagar, a man was reportedly found dead with both his eyes gouged out. The Sindhi Market and Bhanderi Pole areas of Ahmedabad were also reportedly attacked by mobs. India Today reported on 20 May 2002 that there were sporadic attacks on Hindus in Ahmedabad. On 5 May, Muslim rioters attacked Bhilwas locality in the Shah Alam area.

Hindu doctors were asked to stop practicing in Muslim areas after one Hindu doctor was stabbed. Frontline magazine reported that in Ahmedabad, of the 249 bodies recovered by 5 March, thirty were Hindu. Of the Hindus that had been killed, thirteen had died as a result of police action and several others had died while attacking Muslim owned properties. Despite the relatively few attacks by Muslim mobs on Hindu neighborhoods, twenty-four Muslims were reported to have died in police shootings.

The events in Gujarat were the first instance of communal violence in India in the age of 24-hour news coverage and were televised worldwide. This coverage played a central role in the politics of the situation. Media coverage was generally critical of the Hindu right; however, the BJP portrayed the coverage as an assault on the honor of Gujaratis and turned the hostility into an emotive part of their electoral campaign.

With the violence receding in April, a peace meeting was arranged at Sabarmati Ashram, a former home of Mahatma Gandhi. Hindutva supporters and police officers attacked almost a dozen journalists. The state government banned television news channels critical of the government's response, and local stations were blocked. Two reporters working for STAR News were assaulted several times while covering the violence. On a return trip from having interviewed Modi when their car was surrounded by a crowd, one of the crowd claimed that they would be killed if they are the member of a minority community.

The Editors Guild of India, in its report on media ethics and coverage on the incidents stated that the news coverage was exemplary, with only a few minor lapses. The local newspapers Sandesh and Gujarat Samachar, however, were heavily criticized. The report states that Sandesh had headlines which would "provoke, communalize and terrorize people. The newspaper also used a quote from a VHP leader as a headline, "Avenge with blood." The report stated that Gujarat Samachar had played a role in increasing the tensions but did not give all of its coverage over to "hawkish and inflammatory reportage in the first few weeks".

Gujarat Today was given praise for showing restraint and for the balanced reportage of the violence. Critical reporting on the Gujarat government's handling of the situation helped bring about the Indian government's intervention in controlling the violence. The Editors Guild rejected the charge that graphic news coverage aggravated the situation, saying that the coverage exposed the "horrors" of the riots as well as the "supine if not complicit" attitude of the state, helping to propel remedial action.

Many scholars and commentators have accused the state government of being complicit in the attacks, either in failing to exert any effort to quell the violence or for actively planning and executing the attacks themselves. The United States Department of State ultimately banned Narendra Modi from travelling to the United States due to his alleged role in the attacks. These allegations center on several ideas.

First, the state did little to quell the violence, with attacks continuing well through the spring. Further, some attackers used voter lists and other documents obtainable only with government assistance in order to target Muslim communities and households. Moreover, the Vishva Hindu Parishad (VHP), as well as many politicians, including Modi, made inflammatory remarks and endorsed the statewide strike, further stoking tensions.

The historian Gyanendra Pandey described these attacks as state terrorism, saying that they were not riots but "organized political massacres." According to Paul Brass the only conclusion from the evidence which is available points to a methodical Anti-Muslim pogrom which was carried out with exceptional brutality coordination.

In March 2008, the Supreme Court ordered the setting up of a Special Investigation Team (SIT) to reinvestigate the Godhra train burning case and key cases of post-Godhra violence. The former CBI Director R. K. Raghavan was appointed to chair the Team. Christophe Jaffrelot notes that the SIT was not as independent as commonly believed. Other than Raghavan, half of the six members of the team were recruited from the Gujarat police, and the Gujarat High Court was still responsible for appointing judicial officers.

The SIT made efforts to appoint independent prosecutors but some of them resigned due to their inability to function. No efforts were made to protect the witnesses and Raghavan himself was said to be an "absentee investigator," who spent only a few days every month in Gujarat, with the investigations being conducted by the remainder of the team.

As of April 2013, 249 convictions had been secured of 184 Hindus and 65 Muslims. Thirty-one of the Muslim convictions were for the massacre of Hindus in Godhra.The Best Bakery murder trial received wide attention after witnesses retracted testimony in court and all of the accused were acquitted. The Indian Supreme Court, acting on a petition by social activist Teesta Setalvad, ordered a retrial outside Gujarat in which nine accused were found guilty in 2006.

A key witness, Zaheera Sheikh, who repeatedly changed her testimony during the trials and the petition was found guilty of perjury. After police dismissed the case against her assailants, Bilkis Bano approached the National Human Rights Commission of India and petitioned the Supreme Court seeking a reinvestigation. The Supreme Court granted the motion, directing the Central Bureau of Investigation (CBI) to take over the investigation.

CBI appointed a team of experts from the Central Forensic Science Laboratory (CFSL) Delhi and All India Institute of Medical Sciences (AIIMS) under the guidance and leadership of Professor T. D. Dogra of AIIMS to exhume the mass graves to establish the identity and cause of death of victims. The team successfully located and exhumed the remains of victims.

The trial of the case was transferred out of Gujarat and the central government was directed to appoint a public prosecutor. Charges were filed in a Mumbai court against nineteen people as well as six police officials and a government doctor over their role in the initial investigations. In January 2008, eleven men were sentenced to life imprisonment for rapes and murders and a policeman was convicted of falsifying evidence.

The Bombay High Court upheld the life imprisonment of eleven men convicted for the gang rape of Bilkis Bano and murder of her family members during the 2002 Gujarat riots on 8 May 2017. The court also set aside the acquittal of the remaining seven accused in the case, including Gujarat police officers and doctors of a government hospital, who were charged with suppressing and tampering with evidence. Later, the final verdict came on 23 April 2019 as the Supreme Court ordered the Gujarat government to pay Bilkis Yakoob Rasool Bano rupees 50 lakh as compensation, a government job and housing in the area of her choice.

On 3 March 2002, The Prevention of Terrorism Ordinance was invoked against all the accused which was later suspended due to pressure from the Central government. On 9 March 2002, Police added Criminal Conspiracy to the charges. In May 2003, the first charge sheet was filed against 54 accused, but they were not charged under the Prevention of Terrorism Act (POTA became an Act as it was cleared by Parliament). In February 2003, the POTA was re-invoked against all the accused after the BJP retained control of the Gujarat legislature in the 2002 assembly elections.

In November 2003, the Supreme Court of India put a stay on the trial. In 2004, the POTA was repealed after the United Progressive Alliance (UPA) came to power, prompting it to review the invocation of the POTA against the accused. In May 2005, the POTA review commission decided not to charge the accused under POTA. This was later unsuccessfully challenged by a relative of the victim before the Gujarat High Court and later on appeal before Supreme Court.

In September 2008, the Nanavati Commission submitted its report. In 2009, after accepting the report of the Special Investigation Team (SIT) appointed by it, the court appointed a special fast-track court to try the case along with 5 other fast track courts established to try the post-incident riots. The bench hearing the case also said that public prosecutors should be appointed in consultation with the SIT chairman. It ordered that the SIT would be the nodal agency for deciding about witness protection and also asked that it file supplementary charge sheets and that it may cancel the bail of the accused.

More than 100 people were arrested in relation to the incident. The court was set up inside the Sabarmati Central Jail, where almost all of the accused were confined. The hearing began in May 2009. Additional Sessions Judge P R Patel was designated to hear the case. In May 2010, Supreme Court restrained the trial courts from pronouncing judgment in nine sensitive riot cases, including Godhra train incident. The trial was completed in September 2010; however, the verdict could not be delivered because of the Supreme Court stay. The stay was lifted in January 2011 and the judge announced that he shall pronounce the judgment on 22 February 2011.

In February 2011, the trial court convicted 31 people and acquitted 63 others, saying the incident was a planned conspiracy. The convictions were based on the murder and conspiracy provisions of Sections 302 and 120B of the Indian Penal Code respectively and under Sections 149, 307, 323, 324, 325, 326, 332, 395, 397, and 436 of the Code and some sections of the Railway Act and Police Act.[57] The death penalty was awarded to 11 convicts; those believed to have been present at a meeting held the night before the incident where the conspiracy was formed, and those who, according to the court, had actually entered the coach and poured petrol before setting it afire. Twenty others were sentenced to life imprisonment.

Maulvi Saeed Umarji, who was believed by the SIT to be the prime conspirator, was acquitted along with 62 other accused for lack of evidence. The convicted filed appeals in the Gujarat High Court. The state government also challenged the trial court's decision to acquit 61 persons in the High Court and sought death sentences for 20 convicts awarded life imprisonment in the case.

Gujarat High Court changed the death sentence of 11 accused to life imprisonment. All 31 accused found guilty in 2011 were given life imprisonment. 63 accused who were acquitted in 2011 by trial court, were acquitted once again by high court. The court asked the state government and railways to pay 10 lakh rupees compensation to the victims.

Cromosys Publication

Delhi Killings

Niranjan Jha Showman

....

NIRANJAN JHA SHOWMAN

Founder - Niranjan Jha Showman

Education and Technology Research Center

Patankar Park, Nallasopara (W), Mumbai. +91-9561450045

Education, Technology, Publication, Healthcare, Newsmedia, Realtor, Filmmaking

www.facebook.com/cromosys

Cromosys Publication
Teach
Yourself
German
NIRANJAN JHA SHOWMAN

Cromosys Publication

Teach
Yourself
French

NIRANJAN JHA SHOWMAN

Cromosys Publication
Teach
Yourself
Spanish
NIRANJAN JHA SHOWMAN

Cromosys Publication

English
Voice
Accent and
Pronunciation

NIRANJAN JHA SHOWMAN

Teach Yourself Autodesk
MAYA

Cromosys Publication

NIRANJAN JHA SHOWMAN

Cromosys Publication
Teach
Yourself
Autodesk
3ds Max
NIRANJAN JHA SHOWMAN

Cromosys Publication
CRIMINAL FACTORY
NIRANJAN JHA SHOWMAN

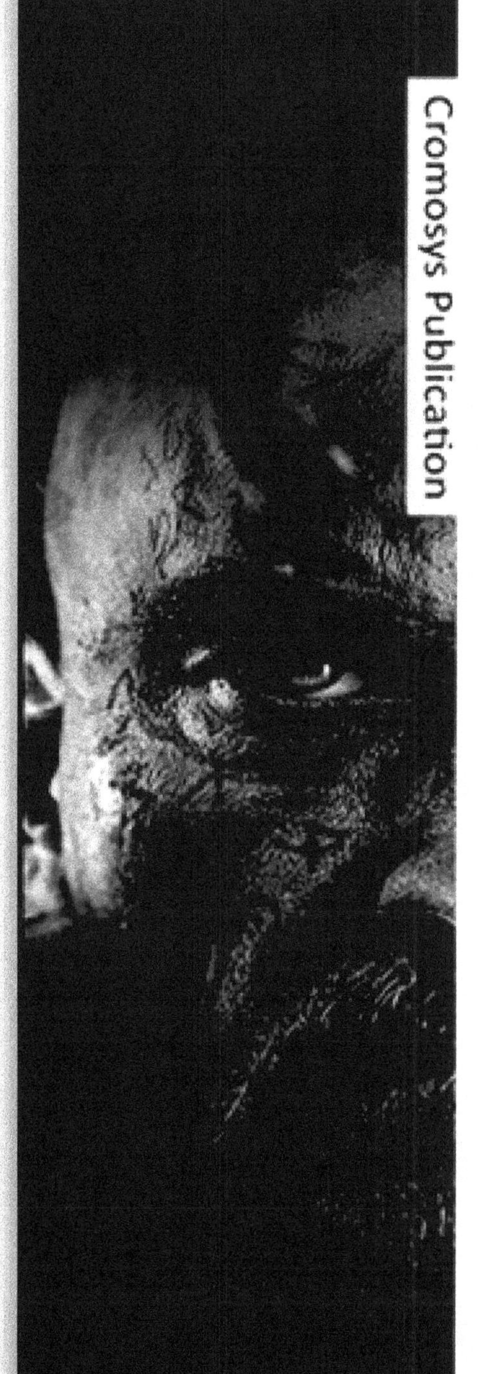

Cromosys Publication
FOCAL DISASTER
NIRANJAN JHA SHOWMAN

Cromosys Publication
Your talents will not help you succeed without your skill of using them.
NIRANJAN JHA SHOWMAN
BE
MILLIONAIRE
LIKE
ME

Read As Much As Possible

www.ingramcontent.com/pod-product-compliance
Lightning Source LLC
Chambersburg PA
CBHW041915130726
48007CB00015B/191